CLIENTS

◈ AND ◈

ADVERSARIES

CLIENTS
AND
ADVERSARIES

A Life at Trial

NOEL GAGE, J.D., M.D.

Wyatt-MacKenzie Publishing
DEADWOOD, OREGON

Clients and Adversaries
A Life at Trial

Noel Gage, J.D., M.D.

Hardcover ISBN: 978-1-942545-81-1
Paperback ISBN: 978-1-942545-88-0

Library of Congress Control Number: 2017941821

Wyatt-MacKenzie Publishing
DEADWOOD, OREGON

Wyatt-MacKenzie Publishing, Inc.
www.WyattMacKenzie.com
Contact us: info@wyattmackenzie.com

Acknowledgments

A special thanks to my grandson David Palmer for his review of the manuscript, his recollection of stories I'd forgotten over the years, and his inspiring me to put my memories on paper in the first place.

Also, thanks to my developmental editor Jerry Payne for his expertise, professionalism, and ability to help me organize my thoughts and stay focused.

Introduction

SOONER OR LATER IN LIFE, you begin to recognize your mortality. From then on, with each passing year, that recognition becomes stronger. As it does so, you naturally start looking back over your life. Mine has been interesting, to say the least. In my career as a trial attorney, I have been blessed with an abundance of often improbable experiences and become acquainted with fascinating people. Many of my friends have heard my funniest and most memorable stories, and many times I have heard someone say to me, "Noel, you ought to write a book!" Finally, I decided to do just that. The result is what you have before you.

Apart from some names that have been changed to preserve the sacred attorney-client privilege, everything herein is as close to fact as memory can serve. I have no axes to grind or agendas to push. My interest in relating these stories is to document them for posterity as accurately as possible.

I trust you'll find some of the episodes funny, some surprising, some dramatic. Hopefully, all of them compelling. For me, it's been fun to revisit these times of my life, and my humble wish is that in reading my accounts of them, you'll find yourself entertained and maybe even a little enlightened. The life of a busy trial attorney can be fairly unpredictable and dull moments are few and far between, a truth that resonated with me all over again in the process of reliving some of these stories.

A profession in law is an honorable pursuit and I feel especially privileged to have made it my career. It has been a long journey from my days at the University of Michigan where I financed my education by driving an ice cream truck for two shifts a day, trying to make ends meet. From those modest days to my days of success and repute in my chosen profession, it seems sometimes as though whole lifetimes have passed. At other times, it all seems like the blink of an eye. What a terrific experience it's been to slow down for a spell to examine it and record it all here. May you enjoy reading it as much as I enjoyed living it.

—Noel Gage
November, 2015

Prologue

"YOU'D HAVE STABBED HIM, too," she explained. "Any-body would have. Especially a lady. No lady wants to be called that word."

"What word is that?" I asked, even though I had a pretty good idea.

She hesitated, then spat it out like a stale piece of gum. "A cunt. Okay? The miserable fucker called me a no-good cunt."

She sat across from me at my boss's desk with trembling hands and long, crossed legs. Her aqua green dress with flow-ing sleeves was cut in a deep V shape down the front, tantalizingly exposing the upper third of her soft, supple breasts. I focused as best I could on her eyes, deep pools of blue set off by the mascara that had run down her cheeks. She was at once vulnerable and defiant. She was, in fact, mag-nificent. I dug down deep for the professionalism the exchange required. It wasn't easy. They hadn't taught us about moments like this in my law courses.

"You say you stabbed him seventeen times?"

"You bet I did, junior. Once for every day we've been living together. I wanted to stab him more."

"What stopped you?"

"The knife broke."

"I see."

"Now look, I came here to see Leonard. Leonard's my

lawyer. Not you."

But it was a Saturday and Leonard wasn't in. Nobody was. It was just me and the sultry creature looking at me with those pleading eyes. The only reason I was there was to take care of some office paperwork. I'd been working for Leonard as a law clerk while finishing up my schooling at the University of Michigan Law School. I had just passed the bar exam. I didn't even have my license to practice yet. Was this my future? Clients barging into the office needing sudden representation for attempted murder charges? Of course maybe if they all looked like her ....

"Would you call him already?" she said. "Would you call Leonard? I really want to talk to him."

"Yes, yes, of course." I dialed up Leonard and told him who was sitting in front of me and why. I told him about the stabbing. The woman's boyfriend had survived and was being treated at Detroit Receiving Hospital. He'd lost a lot of blood but he was going to make it. Leonard knew the woman. He'd represented her before, along with other members of the American Guild of Variety Artists. It sounded like a respectable organization and I guess, in its way, it was. But I'd later learn who most of the members of the venerable AGVA were: strippers and topless dancers.

"Tell her to stay out of sight for the rest of the weekend and I'll surrender her to the Detroit Police Department first thing Monday morning," Leonard advised. I passed along the word to the client who rose and sauntered towards the door.

"See ya, kid," she said over her shoulder. "And thanks for listening."

"Bye, Miss Frank." Her perfume lingered long after she'd closed the door behind her. I sat for some time. I knew I wouldn't be able to get any more work done that day. I decided I'd ask Leonard if he'd let me come along with him first thing Monday for the surrender. I hadn't been to a sur-render before. And I began to realize there were a lot of lawyer things I hadn't done before. Leonard had been mat-ter-of-fact on the phone when I told him about the stabbing. He'd heard it all before. To him, Miss Frank was just another client. Just another person in a jam who needed some legal help. I supposed I'd become matter-of-fact eventually. The legal business would become routine. One case would blend into another.

Looking back now, I can admit that perhaps most of them did. But not all. Some stood out. Some developed and were resolved in most unexpected ways. Some were tragic, some were funny, some were profoundly interesting. And like Miss Frank's perfume, some would be etched into my memory forever.

Table of Contents

CHAPTER ONE

Res Ipsa Loquitur

THE MONDAY MORNING after Miss Frank had come into Leonard's law office and admitted to stabbing her boyfriend seventeen times, I showed up first thing as Leonard had instructed me. We were going to surrender Miss Frank to the Detroit Police Department and I was going to be able to witness the process. But first thing came and went and Leonard hadn't showed. In fact, most of the morning came and went. Leonard finally came through the door at 11:00 a.m.

"Leonard," I said, trying not to sound too disappointed, "I thought you were going to take me along with you when you surrendered Miss Frank. I really wanted to be there."

"Hmm?"

"Miss Frank. The stabbing? The boyfriend? Did you surrender her to the police?"

"Oh, yeah, that. No need. They made up."

"What?"

"The two lovers. They made up. The boyfriend refuses to press charges. It was all a misunderstanding."

"Seventeen stab wounds ..." I said, my voice trailing off.

"Yeah, well, he said he's sorry for calling her a cunt. And before that, he said he'd mowed down her garden. She'd said something that had set him off. And then I guess she got a little pissed off about the garden and that's when things took an ugly turn. One thing led to another. You know how it goes.

Anyway, he's on a lot of pain meds but he was lucid enough to make up with her and the two actually seem pretty happy."

And this was how the Case of the Stabbed Boyfriend turned out. It hadn't become a case at all. The stripper and the boyfriend she'd stabbed until the knife broke were ready to live happily ever after. It was bewildering to me, but that was back in the days when I could actually be surprised by human nature. Time and experience would put an end to that. Looking back, I suppose the complexity and unexpectedness of the human condition is what appealed to me about law in the first place. Or at least it was the reason I had lit out from home several years prior. I wanted to know something about the world, about people, about other places. I wanted to expand my horizons, take some chances, roll the dice.

Back in Queens, my father was a pharmacist. A good one. It was a steady job for a very steady man. My father knew nothing about taking chances. In 1941 he had the opportunity to invest in a new Coca-Cola bottling plant. It required enough intestinal fortitude to part with two hundred dollars, a fortune for us back then, maybe all the money my parents had. Dad passed on it. It was too much of a risk. The plant turned out to be a huge success; my father would have become a very wealthy man. I'd made up my mind that missed opportunities weren't going to be a part of my future.

Back in those days we lived in Brooklyn. It was after second grade that we would move to Queens, my parents and my older brother and I. The Coca-Cola opportunity was long gone by then. But I sensed the world was full of opportunities if you could just get out there and find them. By the time I reached high school, I'd already determined that I was going to get out of New York. I was going to leave the security of home. I wanted to get as far out into the world as I could afford to go.

At first that looked like Harpur College in Endicott—

upstate New York (since moved and renamed; it's now Bing-hamton University). I'd gotten a scholarship to Harpur. But I had two problems with it. It didn't seem to have a lot of cachet (I'd barely heard of it) and it wasn't nearly far enough away. Heck, you could drive there in a single morning. I went west instead, as far as my money would take me: Ann Arbor, Michigan.

There would be no scholarship, however, and tuition and books totaled $1,800 per year, along with another $200 of living expenses. I know it seems like a pittance compared with the cost of higher education today, but back then, money was scarce. My parents could only provide me with the $200. I needed to earn my own way. And so, as soon as I turned eighteen, I got my chauffeur's license, and I spent the summer before my freshman year of college driving a Good Humor truck, selling ice cream.

It was two eight-hour shifts per day, sixteen hours of ringing the Good Humor bell, but I knew it was the only way I could afford to finance my education. I lost track of how many pairs of shoes I wore through jumping in and out of the truck. And there was no time (or money) for lunch and so you availed yourself of the one free ice cream bar you were allowed per shift. Anything more than that and you had to pay out of pocket for it. You prayed for good weather, too. Kids never chased down the ice cream truck in the rain. On days it rained, you waited it out in a diner somewhere, drinking a Coke, maybe eating a hamburger if you decided you were willing to splurge for one. Then you just prayed for sunshine to return.

I became friends with one of the other drivers, an older guy who'd been driving a Good Humor truck forever. Called himself Rosie. Rosie had it all figured out. Rosie would sell ice cream for six months of the year. Then, once it started getting cold and winter began to set in, he considered himself out of a job. He'd file for unemployment, collect the checks, and head down to Florida where he'd spend the winter fishing. Rosie figured he had the system beat. I never met a happier guy. I had slightly higher aspirations, but good for Rosie, I thought.

In any event, it was a long summer for me selling ice cream and I'd repeat it again the next two summers. Two shifts a day. But each summer I was able to make enough money to keep myself in school.

By my sophomore year, I'd met a girl. I was pledging Sigma Alpha Mu and during some pledge initiation high jinks, I found myself being chased by some of the brothers. I managed to escape across the street, ducking into a Hillel Foundation building to hide out, and it was there that I discovered Hilda. Hilda was a year younger and majoring in education. We talked and I asked her out. We hit it off and dated regularly and by the end of my junior year, I'd end up marrying her. I spent that third summer, the summer of 1960, with Hilda, counseling kids at a summer camp in New York.

I had hoped for a different source of summer income. I'd entered a contest to come up with a new slogan for Heinz Ketchup. First prize was $10,000, a fortune back then. Second prize was a station wagon loaded with groceries. I took third prize: a Sunbeam Mixmaster. Not much I could do with that. But in time I learned that Heinz actually used my slogan: "Served in Fine Restaurants." You find a ketchup bottle from those years and you'll most likely see my slogan on it. Unfortunately, I never got anything more from it than the Mixmaster.

By my senior year, Hilda and I had a baby on the way. My responsibilities grew. Now I had to support not only myself, but a family. But whatever job I'd find to make ends meet, I knew it was going to be temporary. I had set my mind on a law career. I was going to be a lawyer.

The idea had first come to me when my parents once found themselves in need of an attorney. Our house in Queens had a retaining wall running along the driveway. Above it was a twenty-foot strip of property owned by the neighbors. When an irrigation system the neighbors installed diverted water from the strip of land, it caused the retaining wall to collapse. It was a mess and clearly the result of the neighbor's actions, but they refused to take responsibility and my parents didn't have the funds needed to rebuild the wall. They hired an attorney who managed to work out a settlement with the neighbors and I became immediately intrigued by how this man was able to use his knowledge of the law to negotiate a deal and help my parents out of a tough spot. Maybe I could help people, too.

After my undergraduate work, I decided to stay where I was and so I enrolled in the University of Michigan Law School. To finance my legal education I managed to land a job selling insurance. I became good at it and the money was sufficient to where I actually considered sticking with it for good. But I didn't consider the matter for long. I knew my future was in law.

It turned out that Hilda's brother-in-law had a good friend who was an attorney: Leonard Lemberg. Leonard needed a clerk and I, finishing my final year of law school, knew I was going to need a foot in the door of my chosen profession. So I began working for Leonard on weekends. Initially, my compensation consisted entirely of free lunch. But that was good enough for me—I was after the practical experience. Leonard and I got along well. He was a good guy, and smart. A great mentor. And when I passed the bar, I went to work for him full time. Leonard paid me a hundred dollars a week.

The problem was that in Michigan, when you passed the bar in November, you had to wait until February to get your license. The bureaucratic wheels move slowly. Three months was too long to wait as far as Leonard was concerned. He had clients whose cases were coming to trial and he didn't have time to try them all himself. For one thing, he had a hobby that kept him busy: cars. At any given time he'd have as many as eight of them, all beautiful classics that he kept in top shape. But it was not unusual for him to drive into work on Monday in a car he hadn't owned the previous Friday. So Leonard needed me. "Let's get you admitted to the bar, kid," he said one day.

"How are you gonna do that?"

"Don't worry, I'll take care of it." Leonard went to the courthouse and filed a motion. He had clients who were counting on me, he said in the motion. They'd waited long enough for proper representation. Justice delayed is justice denied. My not having my law license was creating a hardship. The bar would have to make an exception.

Leonard's motion was granted. Of all my friends who had passed the bar, I was the first to start practicing. Two full months before any of them.

And Leonard wasted no time getting me into the game. He had clients and they needed legal help.

"Here," he said, almost immediately after he'd secured my license.

"What's this?" I said.

"The file for your first case. You go before the judge in Common Pleas court this afternoon."

"What? Leonard, I don't even know where the Common Pleas court is."

"Don't worry about it, kid. The client will show you. And

he'll fill you in on the case. It's pretty straightforward. Good luck! I'm off to check out a car I've had my eye on."

With that, Leonard walked out of the office, leaving me alone with the file for my very first case. Shortly after that, the client walked in: Malcolm McKinstry, wealthy developer, builder of most of the prisons in the state of Michigan. A real success story. And to my great fortune, a genuinely nice guy.

We walked the four blocks from Leonard's office to the courthouse while I read the file Leonard had given me and listened to McKinstry as he described his cause of action.

"It happened with the night depository machine at the bank," he began. "I made a deposit one night after hours. I slipped it into the box and the jaws of the damn thing closed on my hand as I pulled my hand out. I couldn't believe it. Cut my finger pretty badly. I needed stitches. Had to go to the hospital. Hey, look, sometimes things happen and I understand that. But all I wanted was the bank to acknowledge their machine caused an injury. Pay for my trip to the doctor, you know? So the next day I went in to see the branch manager and I told him what had happened and he looked at me like I was some kind of scam artist. 'I'm sorry, we can't help you,' he said and then he just walked away. And you know the funny thing? I'm that bank's biggest depositor and the manager didn't even recognize me."

We walked into the courthouse as I formulated my plan. I didn't take three years of law school for my health. This was my first case and I wasn't about to lose it. In my mind, it was a slam dunk. *Res ipsa loquitur*, I thought. The thing speaks for itself. The very fact that the accident happened raised an inference of negligence. The bank owned the machine and the machine caused an injury through no fault of my client. Therefore, the bank was negligent. Simple, logical, undeniable. I was pretty pleased with myself for the legal strategy

I'd mapped out.

We entered the courtroom and waited for the judge, who strode in shortly and immediately greeted the bank's attorney.

"Bob!" the judge said. "How the heck are you? How's your short game these days?"

"Bob" smiled and said something about "our next time out on the links" and then the judge looked at me.

"What's your name, kid?"

"Noel Gage, Your Honor."

"Well, Noel Gage, what have you got for me today?" I explained the facts of the case and then I put McKinstry on the stand. I questioned him, essentially having him repeat for the judge what he'd told me on the way to the courthouse. He went through the whole incident—the malfunctioning depository machine, the stitches, everything. And then, my confidence level rising, I described my theory of *res ipsa loquitur*. Certainly, I thought, the judge would have to come to the same conclusion I had come to.

The judge sat expressionless throughout. For the bank's part, "Bob" simply asked for a dismissal. Then the judge turned to me and said, "Okay, counsel, I've heard your case. I find no grounds for it. Judgment for defendant." Then he rose and walked out. Just like that, swiftly, casually, the judge had launched my legal career with an ego-bruising loss. I was devastated.

"Mr. McKinstry," I said, turning to my client, "I'm really sorry ... I don't know what ... how ... I mean, my strategy ...."

"Hey, don't worry about it, kid!" McKinstry laughed, slapping me on the back. "You were great. I like the way you handled yourself. We made our point. Besides, the joke's on those bastards anyway. This morning I pulled all my money out of the bank. I won; they just don't know it yet."

We walked out of the courthouse while I tried to smile and pretend that I wasn't hopelessly demoralized about myself and what I had chosen as my life's work.

CHAPTER TWO

The Right Profession

BACK AT THE OFFICE, Leonard listened to me recount the events of my first trial with a sympathetic ear. He sensed my dejection. "Look, you didn't do anything at all wrong," he assured me. "You had the right legal theory. In fact it was a great theory. But you know what you didn't have?"

"What's that?"

"A friendship with the judge. He and the bank's attorney? They're golfing buddies. Legal theories notwithstanding, you never stood a chance, kid." It was a valuable lesson. From that point forward, I determined never to put the fate of a client in the hands of a judge. I would ask for jury trials where impartial citizens would decide my cases. It's the kind of lesson they don't teach you in law school. In law school, for the most part, it's conceptual and theoretical. My experiences with Leonard, experiences in the actual world of law, were where I was getting the real education.

Law school had been long and hard. Which is why, shortly after graduation, before the Case of the Golfing-Buddy Judge, three friends and I had decided we'd earned the right to celebrate with a little rest and relaxation in sunny Florida. The trip, however, didn't exactly turn out to be very restful *or* relaxing.

I didn't drink at the time but my friends did and, during that celebratory trip, moderation of alcohol intake wasn't a high priority. It all came to a head one night at the Doral Hotel in Miami. After dinner and way too many drinks, the bill came and since I was the only sober one, it was left to me to figure out what everyone owed. But the bill didn't look quite right to me. The itemized list was correct, but the bottom line was off. Way off, it seemed to me. After doing the math, I determined the bill was exactly one hundred dollars too high and I knew it was no accident. The waiter hadn't realized there was a sober customer at his table and had taken the opportunity to add a hundred bucks to the bill. He'd run it through the adding machine properly, but then he'd slipped the tape out of the machine, added in the hundred, and then slipped the tape back in before he totaled it. In my sobriety, I caught it. The other guys never would have. But then I had to tell them what happened.

"This guy's trying to rip us off," I said, and that's when all hell broke loose.

My three buddies stood in unison and flipped the table over, dishes and glasses crashing to the floor. I looked around to see the stunned faces of the other customers. Then the three moved toward the waiter. I don't know what would have happened had I not been there to get between the guys and the waiter but I can't imagine it would have been too good for any of us, the waiter in particular.

"*Guys!*" I said, "C'mon, we just graduated law school! How's it going to look if we tear this place up and beat the hell out of this guy? Didn't we just learn that you can't be judge, jury, and executioner?" For the waiter's part, he had the look of a man in fear for his very life, which, now that I think about it, was fairly appropriate, given the situation. I managed to get the guys settled down and, in the end, we got out of there with no bloodshed and I left the exact amount of the bill less one hundred dollars. Not a single penny more for a tip.

At any rate, we began making our way back home the next day and we all eventually went our separate ways in life. I lost track of one of those guys over the years but remained good friends with another one and we even considered forming a firm together. The idea was scuttled when we couldn't agree on whose name would go first. A silly concern, in hindsight. He went on to become a circuit judge. The third friend ended up moving to California. He'd been a successful lawyer in Detroit but had to leave after being shot by a Mafioso type who didn't care for the fact that my friend had slept with his wife.

⤙

Back at Leonard's, I was getting an education about human nature. One afternoon the phone rang. I took the call and listened as a man spoke about wanting to sue a famous food manufacturing company that had made the applesauce he'd just purchased at his local grocery store.

"There's glass in the jar!" he declared.

"Hmm ... did you cut yourself on it?" I asked.

"Well, no."

"Did you ingest any of it?"

"No. But I mean ... there's glass in the jar!" he repeated.

"I understand," I said, "but I'm afraid that without any damages, there's nothing I can really do. Now, if you'd taken a spoonful of it and tried to eat it and cut the inside of your mouth or tongue or something, then maybe you'd have a cause of action. Then you'd have damages, you see. All I can recommend is that you take the jar back to wherever you got it for a replacement or a refund."

13

The man thanked me but I could tell he was disappointed.

An hour later, he called back.

"Mr. Gage!" he said, "Good news! I tried to eat the applesauce and it cut my mouth up pretty bad. I'm bleeding! How much do you think we can get?" If he was disappointed the first time he hung up, the disappointment was dwarfed by his chagrin after being told he had injured himself for nothing.

"I can't help you," I had to tell him. "I'd lose my license to practice." Now, I don't know if he called another attorney but I never heard anything more from him. But I sat in the office after the call wondering if people wanting to sue applesauce companies for bogus reasons were going to represent the bulk of my future clientele. At that point, it had been $100 a week from Leonard to field that kind of calls. Truthfully, I'd been making more money from the insurance job I'd taken to get me through law school. This was beginning to seem like a step backwards.

⌒

At the insurance agency, I sold health and accident for American Income Life Insurance Company and I'd done well, making even more money than my law school professors were making. Technically, if you had a part-time job during law school you had to get permission from the dean. I didn't even bother to try. I had more than a part-time job. Not only was I working for American Income Life, I was clerking for Leonard and I also worked for a time in the city attorney's office. I had three part-time jobs. There was no way I could imagine that permission would be granted so I just kept my mouth shut about my extra-curricular activities.

I had found the insurance position in an ad I saw in the local paper: *Teachers Wanted for Insurance Sales.* I guess teachers were considered smart enough to pass the insurance license test and a lot of them were looking for part-time work, too, especially in the summers. The teaching profession was a good source of employees. I called the number in the ad and said, "I'm not a teacher, but I'm sure I can do anything a teacher can do." The man chuckled and told me to come on in, and after an obligatory interview, I was hired and was soon out selling insurance to anyone I could find who was buying.

Quickly I learned how much money there must be in the insurance industry. The compensation structure for a whole life policy was such that I'd get fifty percent of the customer's first-year premiums. My manager would get twenty percent and his manager would get thirty-five percent. That means that 105% of the first-year premium would go to sales commission and I realized just how much profit there must be in whole life insurance for the company to be willing to forego the premiums, and even come out of pocket, for an entire year after the sale of a policy.

During the course of selling insurance, I'd had the good fortune to meet an engineering student named Ruben. Ruben was from Caracas and his Venezuelan family was wealthy. In fact, they were known as the Rockefellers of Caracas. Hilda and I would go from time to time to visit Ruben at his place in Ann Arbor, where he lived with his wife Sally. They'd often have other guests, Venezuelan friends of theirs. One of them was a man by the name of Luis. Luis and I became friends, too, and Luis would eventually go on to become head of the Venezuelan armed services in the 1960s. All of Ruben's friends had money and they all bought insurance from me, boosting my income and my status in the company. I won some sales contests and one time even a diamond ring.

In my senior year of law school, American Income Life offered me a full-time position. The job came with a good salary and a Buick convertible. Plus performance bonuses. I thought seriously about it, but I knew that in the long run, law was the avenue with the most potential. But it sure didn't seem like it sitting that day in Leonard's office explaining to a man with a bleeding mouth why I couldn't represent him.

⌐

The Applesauce Case was followed not long after by a collections case. Leonard had won a judgment from a large grocery store chain; but as I'd come to learn, winning doesn't always mean collecting. The chain had neglected to pay. Leonard handed me the file one day.

"Here," he said. "Collect this judgment, okay?"

"How do I do that?"

"You went to law school. Figure it out."

Things weren't getting any better. But I did a little research and asked around and determined how best to proceed. I secured a writ of execution, an order from the court to collect payment. It included the services of the sheriff's office to take possession of the debtor's property if necessary. Then I drove out to one of the stores, accompanied by two deputies and a truck. The three of us walked in and I asked for the manager and produced the writ. The manager was unmoved by the show of force.

"Take it up with the main office," he said. But of course that had already been done and to no avail. Apparently a clerical error at the main office was preventing payment. We'd gotten nowhere. Now I was left with no choice.

"Okay, gentlemen," I said to the deputies. "Start taking it away."

"Start taking what away?" said the manager.

"Non-perishables, please," I motioned to the deputies. And said to the manager, "Whatever we need to pay this debt. That's what the writ of execution is for. Now, I'll leave it up to the deputies to decide on the specific items." The deputies, meanwhile, had already decided. Seems that doing their jobs didn't necessarily have to mean doing any heavy lifting. They looked around for the lightest store items they could confiscate and began walking armloads of toilet paper out of the front of the store towards the truck. I assumed rolls of paper towels were next.

"Okay, okay!" said the manager. "Hold on. Let me call the main office." He trotted back to his desk at the rear of the store and five minutes later he was pulling the amount of the judgment out of the store's safe. With cash in hand, we returned the toilet paper.

Fortunately, not long after the Applesauce Case and the Collections Case, I received a call that seemed a little more like what I'd had in mind when I decided to become a lawyer in the first place. A man had purchased a can of tuna fish and in the course of eating the tuna fish, he noticed a half-eaten fly in the can. It didn't take him long to apprehend where the other half of the fly had gone. Just the thought of it made him violently ill. A couple days of general nausea followed. Unlike the Applesauce plaintiff, this poor guy had a legitimate reason to sue, it seemed to me, and so I took the case.

We went to Common Pleas court and this time I insisted on a jury. No judges for me anymore. In Common Pleas court, the jury consisted of a total of six men and women. I decided that my strategy with the jury needed to be more than just questioning my client on the witness stand to present the basic facts of the case. I knew I needed to do more. I needed to paint a picture for the jury, make them understand what eating that fly really meant to my client. I needed an emotional, visceral reaction.

"Ladies and gentlemen of the jury," I began. "One has to ask oneself what the full ramifications are of knowing you ingested a fly, as my client unfortunately did. Where, I am compelled to ask, do flies come from? Where does one find flies? They start as maggots, of course, feeding on feces and all forms of vile and putrid and disgusting things. And they spend their short lives continuing to feed on garbage and waste and spoiled foods and excrement. You'll find them in dumpsters and sewers and buzzing around the decayed and rotting corpses of animals—rodents and rats and the dead possum by the side of the road putrefying in the hot sun."

By then I noticed a couple jurors turning a slight shade of green. One involuntarily put a hand to her mouth. I knew it was time to hit them with the knockout punch: "And my client had one of those things in his mouth. *In his mouth*, ladies and gentlemen!"

It didn't hurt that I had preserved the can of tuna and brought it with me as evidence. I wasn't exactly sure how I was going to make use of it, but the question soon took care of itself. The can had been in a plastic bag in my freezer for the weeks leading up to the trial. But in the stuffy courtroom on that hot summer day, it hadn't taken long for the tuna to putrefy, or for the stench to waft through the courtroom and into the judge's nose, prompting this outburst: "Mr. Gage, kindly take that goddamn can *out* of my courtroom!"

The jury didn't deliberate very long before returning a verdict in favor of my client. My strategy had worked. I don't know; it was probably the kind of case I would never have taken in my later days as a lawyer, bordering as it did perhaps on the frivolous side. But at the time, it was a good learning experience and I felt great about getting a judgment for a client who really had been sickened by the thought of that fly.

Other cases followed. Even better ones. I was learning quickly and gaining a lot of experience. My confidence was growing, too. Soon I was taking on at least a couple cases a week. On one particular day I had a trial in the morning and another in the afternoon. Before long, I became an associate in Leonard's firm and instead of the $100 a week, I began receiving fifty percent of whatever the firm took in from my cases. In Common Pleas court, the maximum amount of an award was only $3,000, but we'd take a third and I'd get half of that. Good money in those days and it added up.

Fortunately, the cases were pretty simple and straight-forward and when they'd go to court, the trial might not last more than a couple of hours. Sometimes the longest part of the process was picking a jury. That might take longer than the trial itself. But I was learning that it was just as important, if not more so, and I became good at it, getting a sense quickly as to which jury candidates would be most sympathetic to my clients. From there, the trick was to develop that sympathy. Tug on the heartstrings.

Case in point: a man came to me after having been in a traffic accident. He was a Polish immigrant with a family of eight and very little money. He sat across my desk and pulled out a doctor bill for five dollars. The bill didn't exactly seem to me as though it represented a lot of damages.

"Your medical bill for the accident only came to five dollars?" I asked.

"No sir," he replied. "That's the only bill I can afford. The rest I cannot handle. I have no money to return to the doctor. And I cannot work. My family needs my paycheck but I cannot work in my injured condition and I cannot afford any medical help."

I took the case.

The man had come to the office with his whole family and I interviewed each member, trying to get everyone's unique perspective. Of all the family members, I was struck most by the sincerity and innocence of the man's ten-year-old son. I knew he could provide the sympathy and heart-tug I needed.

When the case made its way to trial, I questioned the boy on the stand about the accident, about the injuries to his father, about how his father could no longer work, about how his father was the breadwinner of the family, and about how his father could not afford a doctor. The kid was straightforward and genuine. The jury was eating it up. Then came the cross-examination from the defense attorney.

"Did you talk to your lawyer before you took the stand, young man?"

"Yes, sir," the boy said.

"I see," he smiled knowingly, glancing at the jury box. "And did he tell you just what to say?"

The boy turned and faced the jury. "Mr. Gage told me to just tell the truth. And if I did that, the jury would take good care of my daddy."

It was perfect. The defense attorney's smile withered away and he quickly made the decision that his best course of action was to get the kid off the stand.

"No more questions," he said.

I rested my case. When the jury delivered their verdict, they awarded the family the maximum—$3,000. That was the moment I knew it for certain: I was in the right profession after all.

CHAPTER THREE

My Stock in Trade

OF ALL THAT I learned in those early days with Leonard, perhaps nothing was as important as the value of creativity and imagination. Many cases, I came to understand, were problems in need of inventive solutions. I became a problem solver. So it was in the Case of the Union Picnic. Some eighty people contracted food poisoning at a local AFL-CIO picnic that had been catered by an area restaurant. Collectively, they wanted to sue the restaurant and they came to me to represent them. I made contact with the restaurant's attorney in the hopes of a settlement. His response? Laughter.

"Where are the damages?" he said. "People didn't feel well for a day or two?" He had a point. Sure, the people had been sickened, but the illnesses, though uncomfortable, were short-lived, none of them resulting in anything more than inconvenience. But I was hired to do a job and I intended to find a way to do it. It was a problem in need of an inventive solution.

And then an idea hit me. If it were an insurance matter, each person would have to file their claim separately. So why not take a page out of the insurance industry's book and file each suit separately? If successful, I'd get a lot more money for my clients on an individual rather than collective basis. But more important, who wants to go to court eighty times? For the restaurant, it would be death by a thousand cuts. The strategy worked. The restaurant managed to hang in there for all of two cases before agreeing to a settlement.

⤿

In time, I moved on from Leonard's. In the course of my trial work, I'd met many lawyers and eventually I formed a partnership with some of them. The partnership would change over time, with partners leaving and other partners joining, but over the course of years, I was privileged to work with, among others, Marty Doctoroff (whose son Daniel was the head of Bloomberg up until 2014); Mark Reizen, who's had an illustrious career and continues to be involved in the legal profession; George Bushnell Jr., son of a Michigan Supreme Court justice and who would ultimately become president of the American Bar Association; and S. John Byington who would go on to be appointed by President Gerald Ford as Chairman of the Consumer Product Safety Commission. It was an impressive group of guys.

But I didn't exactly leave Leonard. I brought him with me and we gave him an office and an "Of Counsel" status. It was the least I could do for the man who gave me my start.

George Bushnell brought a lot to the table when he came aboard. I'd gotten to know him during a case where my law firm itself was in need of representation. You never represent yourself, of course. We hired George's firm. At that time, he was president of the Michigan State Bar Association. We enjoyed our working relationship and George decided to leave the large law firm he'd been with and join us.

George was quite a character. A big man, over six feet and somewhere around three hundred pounds, he was articulate and delivered his words with a booming voice. George was also a fan of Glenlivet Single Malt Scotch and could be quite gregarious and outgoing. His eventual election as president of the American Bar Association came partly by way of him traveling around, meeting many attorneys and entertaining them with dinners and drinks, and I used to joke with him that he drank his way to the presidency. But in truth nobody was better suited for the job. George wasn't afraid of speaking his mind. Once, during an ABA national convention addressing Congress's plan to slash funding to the Legal Services Corporation, a non-profit organization formed to assist poor people in finding legal help, George called the House representatives "reptilian bastards"—a phrase that drew the ire of the House, but also became something of a popular expression. If you hear any of our illustrious members of Capitol Hill ever referred to as reptilian bastards, you'll know where it began.

Most of George's work had been as a product liability attorney for a major automobile manufacturer. The cases would come to him through Herzfeld and Rubin in New York, arguably the top product liability firm in the world. They represented the manufacturer throughout the United States, appointing lawyers wherever there would be a case against their client. Herzfeld and Rubin relied on experienced trial attorneys and trained them in the intricacies of lawsuits against the car manufacturer. Once George joined us, we began working with Herzfeld and Rubin on Michigan cases. They had offices in New Jersey, California, and Florida. Eventually, after George left for the ABA, we merged with them and became Gage, Herzfeld, and Rubin in Michigan. For cases in our state, I became the go-to guy.

A lot of the cases were sudden acceleration cases—cars presumably speeding up for no reason. I can't say that sudden acceleration caused by a manufacturing defect has never been a factor in a car accident, but all I saw in my time with these cases was driver error. The burden of proof, of course, was on the plaintiffs. And although they'd bring in engineers to try to prove design fault, we were always able to shake their testimony. There was one particular engineer who traveled around the country making a career out of testifying for plaintiff attorneys. But I was trained well by Herzfeld and Rubin, as well as by the manufacturer, and I'd become extremely knowledgeable about the design and manufacturing of these cars. I began to feel like an engineer myself. I knew the questions to ask and I knew if the answers were off the beam. Consequently, I was able to shake the traveling engineer so badly on the stand during one cross-examination that I don't believe he ever testified anywhere again. We had a total of forty-two sudden acceleration cases and we won every single one of them.

Of course the cases against the car manufacturer weren't always about sudden acceleration. Some were about the ability of the cars to safely withstand accidents. And they weren't always legitimate. Like the time a plaintiff filed suit seeking damages in the millions because a car accident had rendered him, so he claimed, unable to participate in the two major passions of his life: golf and sex. Had the car been made better, he argued, he would not have been so severely injured. Now his life, as he knew it, was effectively over.

I knew a phony when I saw one. As for the sex, I had a nurse working for us who did a little research into the plaintiff's true condition.

"Sir," I said during my cross-examination of the man, "You claim you cannot have sexual intercourse as a result of the car accident, is that correct?"

"That's correct."

"And yet, don't you suffer from an unrelated condition that prevents you from having sexual intercourse?"

"An unrelated condition? Well, I, uh ... I don't know if

... I'm sure I don't know what you mean ...."

"Isn't it true that you suffer from a condition known as Peyronie's Disease?"

"Well, I mean, yeah, but ...."

"And for the benefit of the jury, would you mind explaining what Peyronie's Disease is?"

The man looked down, clearly embarrassed, then quietly mumbled something.

"I'm sorry, sir, would you mind repeating that a little louder?" I said.

"Peyronie's Disease," he sighed, "is ... well, it's a severe curvature of the penis."

"I see. And isn't it more likely that the curvature of your penis is what is preventing you from having sexual intercourse?"

"Well, I suppose it's possible but, look, I was severely injured in that accident. I mean, c'mon. I can't play golf anymore. I can't swing the club at all like I used to be able to."

His changing the subject I took to be a concession that the Peyronie's Disease, not the car accident, was at the root of the sex problem. I could sense the jury felt the same way just from their suppressed laughter and so I was happy to change gears along with him. My point had been made. Now it was time to make another point. As it happened, I had managed to plant, unnoticed, a nine-iron under the defense table before the trial had gotten underway that morning.

"Yes, about the golf," I said. "Certainly it's tragic that you cannot swing the club as before. Anyone who plays golf can surely understand your frustration."

"Thank you," he said, apparently grateful for my understanding words.

"Now," I continued, pulling out the nine-iron, "just for the edification of the jury, would you mind stepping down here and showing all of us the way in which you used to be able to swing the club?"

"I'd be glad to!" he smiled, bouncing off the stand and swiping the club from my hand. "Okay, before the accident, I could do this," and he proceeded to make a perfect swing, bringing the club up above his shoulder and then slicing it downward, cutting through the air with a *swoosh* and ending with a flawless follow-through. Arnold Palmer could not have done it better. "See? Notice that form? Here, I'll do it again." Another perfect swing. *Swoosh!* "Now that's the way I *used* to be able to do it! But now I can't do it that ... uh ... now when I swing the ... um ...."

Slowly the problem with his demonstration was dawning on him. He handed the club back to me and slunk back to the witness chair with an expression of complete resignation. I glanced at his attorney who was slumping down in his seat so far it seemed he might actually go under the table, which I imagine is where he would have preferred to have been.

"No more questions," I said. Needless to say, the case was dismissed.

Some cases for the car manufacturer weren't so easy. Some were much more involved. A husband and wife and their four children were in a terrible accident that rendered both parents quadriplegics. It was a tragic accident to be sure and you're never happy having to view the victims of tragedy as opponents. But the fact is the man had driven their van into a concrete viaduct at a high rate of speed. There wasn't a car on earth that could have withstood the impact. And during a deposition, the man admitted he had been arguing with his wife at the time. Moreover, it turns out he had a criminal background, was frequently drunk, and was an abusive husband and father, one time even threatening his kids with a knife. Moments before the accident, he had taken a swing at his wife in the front seat of the car causing him to lose control of the vehicle. There was just no way that the car manufacturer bore any responsibility for the accident's outcome. Nevertheless, the judge in the case was not exactly sympathetic to big auto makers (nor especially knowledgeable about legal history as I would soon come to discover) and I knew we'd still have our work cut out for us.

The plaintiff's attorneys, grasping at straws, were seeking to depose one of the car manufacturer's engineers in West Germany. There was only one problem with that, and I knew it. According to the Hague Evidence Convention, a treaty that governs international cooperation in civil law, it was illegal for a foreign lawyer to depose a German national on German's own soil. It was a well-respected and—at least I had assumed—well-known law. This put me between the proverbial rock and hard place. If I participated in the deposition, I'd be violating international law. If I chose not to attend the deposition, I wouldn't be properly representing the client. I went before the judge to argue that the deposition should not take place:

"It's a violation of the Hague Convention!"

"Mr. Gage," the judge began, "Judge Hague from traffic court holds no influence here. Now, I don't care how he does things in his courtroom or what his conventions or standards are. This is *my* courtroom and *I* will make the decisions as to who gets deposed and where. Do we understand each other?"

I stood open-mouthed for a moment and then collected myself.

"But, your honor –"

"Do we *understand* each other, Mr. Gage? Now, I advise you to get yourself to Germany to properly represent your client. In fact, I insist on it. Failure to do so will very much tempt me to enter a default judgment and we'll just leave it up to the jury to decide on the amount of damages. The choice is yours."

So much for my motion to the judge. I flipped a coin with another attorney on the case (there were probably half a dozen of us on this one) to see who would go to Germany and risk an illegal deposition and who would stay to file an appeal. It came up heads and the other attorney headed for the airport. I headed for the court of appeals, which did exactly nothing, forcing me to file an emergency motion with the Michigan Supreme Court. They sat on it as well. Everyone seemed apparently satisfied with the judge's directive, notwithstanding the protocols of the Hague Convention. We had only one remaining place to go: the United States Supreme Court.

Two of us from the firm flew to Washington, D.C. and filed our motion. This time we got some attention. Justice Sandra Day O'Connor was on the circuit at the time and she granted us the order we were looking for. Her opinion confirmed that the Hague Convention could not be violated. The deposition could not take place.

The plaintiff's attorneys took a look at the ruling and here is where *they* became imaginative. I wasn't the only one looking for inventive solutions. They had cards to play, too. "We'll depose the engineer in Germany," they said, "but at the U.S. Embassy. That's American soil."

Whether or not they had a legitimate argument, who knows? But it seemed to me that their strategy was a clear attempt at circumventing the intent of the relevant portion of the Hague Convention. And it was back in front of the judge to argue it once again. I didn't get very far.

"Mr. Gage," the judge said, "I thought I told you last time that I care nothing whatsoever about the manner in which

Judge Hague runs his particular courtroom. Your motion is denied."

From there, it was back to the appeals court (which did nothing again), then back to the Michigan Supreme Court (which also did nothing again) and, finally, back to Justice O'Connor who, fortunately for us, didn't seem too interested in interpreting and defining the subtle points of the Hague Convention. Her ensuing opinion was unmistakable in its perturbation for having to even reconsider the ruling, especially after the Michigan Supreme Court sat on the motion not once, but now twice: "The failure of the Michigan Supreme Court to act promptly should not prevent a member of this Court from entertaining an application to stay the order."

In the end, we settled the case for an amount so low we considered it a huge victory. The accident, notwithstanding the horrendous consequences of it, was clearly the fault of the driver and no amount of engineering, given the recklessness and high rate of speed, could have produced a different outcome. I don't think the deposition of the engineer would have made much of a difference one way or the other but sometimes the seemingly ancillary issues on a complex case can be the most time-consuming and it becomes important to win them. Every little battle sets a tone. Every little victory takes you one step closer to a favorable verdict or a favorable settlement. And it's particularly gratifying to get a favorable opinion from a justice of the United States Supreme Court.

And just for the record, I never did have any knowledge as to what goes on in Judge Hague's traffic court.

〜

Though we were extraordinarily successful representing

the automobile manufacturer, I can't stipulate without exception that cars, even those designed by our client, are always
as safe as they can be. Cars are designed by human beings
after all. But one thing I will stipulate: like most products,
you're going to have a much harder time proving you've been
unnecessarily put at risk if you've somehow altered the car.
And the bigger the alteration, the worse it's going to be for
you. Case in point: The Case of the Junkyard Auto.

The suit was filed by a man who had suffered grievous
bodily harm in an accident and had incurred massive medical
bills. The claim was that the automobile was not "crash worthy." Had the vehicle been designed better, his injuries would
not have been as serious. As with all our cases, I did a thorough
investigation, which naturally included a complete inspection
of the vehicle. For that, I made use of an investigator who
carefully and methodically examined the damaged car, taking
lots of photographs from various angles. Sifting through the
photos, we noticed something curious, something we brought
up at the trial.

"Mr. Jones," I asked the man during cross-examination
when the case ultimately made its way to court, "is this photo
a picture of your wrecked automobile?" I had projected a
photo of his car onto a large screen at the front of the courtroom.

"Yes, it certainly is."

"And how about this one here?"

"Yep."

"And if we go back to the first one and zoom in, can you
see, right there on the dashboard, the vehicle identification
number?"

"Sure, I see it."

"Would you mind reading it to the jury?" To which the
plaintiff happily read the letters and numbers of the VIN.

"And now if we go back to the second photo," I continued, "representing the rear of the car, this time stamped onto the axle there's another VIN number. Can you see that?"

"Sure."

"And might I trouble you to read that one aloud to the jury?"

The man suddenly began to fidget nervously in his seat. His voice went so low that the judge had to ask him to speak up. Five characters into the VIN, it became apparent to everybody in the courtroom what had happened. The second set of numbers was different than the first one he'd read. A few more uncomfortable questions and the truth came out. The plaintiff's car had been pieced together from two different cars, the rear assembly of one car having been welded onto the back of another. For all we knew, there might have even been a third vehicle somewhere in the plaintiff's Frankenstein of a car. The case was summarily dismissed.

Professionally, I was enjoying my time as a products liability attorney and I loved the big cases. Each had its own distinct set of challenges to overcome. And whether or not the solution was in the close inspection of vehicle identification numbers, the respected opinion of a Supreme Court justice, or the well-timed presentation of a nine-iron, surmounting the challenges for ultimate victory was always gratifying, always rewarding. The cases were problems in need of inventive solutions. And inventive solutions had become my stock in trade.

CHAPTER FOUR

Dangerous People

CLIENTS ARE ALWAYS GRATEFUL, of course, when you win a case for them, but some are more grateful than others. Of all the clients who ever expressed gratitude for my work, one stands out not so much for his expression of thanks (although that certainly stands out), but for the fact that this client, when he first approached me, let me know in no uncertain terms how he felt about my profession; gratitude from this guy was something I could never in a million years have anticipated.

"I hate all fucking lawyers," were the first words out of his mouth after he'd introduced himself. "Just thought you should know."

"Thanks," I said. "Can I ask why you're here?"

"'Cause I need a lawyer"

"I see."

"But I've been in business fifty years and I've been sued a number of times—never justifiably and I've lost every single suit. So it's nothing personal, but I hope you can see why I feel the way I do. Lawyers. I just fucking hate 'em."

"Well, maybe I can do better for you."

And it turns out I did do better. I defended him successfully from a frivolous lawsuit, his first victory in court, if I'm to believe his claim that he always (unjustifiably) lost. The jury's decision in our favor came by way of my cross-examination of the plaintiff.

"Wow," my curmudgeonly client said when I returned to the defense table after my cross. "You got that guy's head on a platter!"

"Shush," I whispered. "The jury can hear you, probably the judge, too."

"On a *platter!*" he repeated.

A year went by. Then one day, the client showed up in our lobby insisting on seeing me. I came out and there he was, holding a big long package wrapped in butcher paper. I couldn't imagine what could be inside.

"Noel," he said, "I never thanked you properly for defending me last year. You did a terrific job. You single-handedly restored my faith in our justice system. And so I wanted to offer you something in appreciation. Here. Hope you like it."

I unwrapped the paper and underneath was a nearly five-foot-tall papier-mâché statue of the plaintiff I had cross-examined, signed by Stephen Hansen, famous in the art world for his playful and humorous depictions of human personality. The representation of the plaintiff was perfect—the suit he wore, his eyes, his long nose, even the dots on the tie he wore that day. Obviously my client must have snapped a picture of the plaintiff, even though cameras were strictly forbidden in the courtroom. Then he commissioned Hansen to create the uncanny likeness. And the best part? Attached to the back of the plaintiff's neck, between his head and shoulders, was a silver platter.

I stared for several moments at the creation, then turned to thank the client. But he was gone. I tried to follow him, taking the elevator down to the entrance of the building and out into the street, but the client was nowhere to be found. Just like that, he had disappeared. In fact, I would never see him again. But I kept the Hansen and I've even collected a few more since then, none quite so meaningful, however, as the one from the client who started out hating "all fucking lawyers." I know for a fact that, wherever this client is, there's at least one lawyer he doesn't mind so much.

⌒

Ah, but not everybody you come in contact with appreciates what you do. Some people are rude, some ignorant, some boorish. And some are just plain dangerous.

You don't really expect the dangerous kind when you're working on product liability cases. The cases are normally pretty straightforward and without a lot of drama. For the automobile manufacturer, for instance, we'd typically have somebody injured in a crash who wanted to sue the company and it was our job to represent the company. It was just business. These were civil proceedings and the people involved were, for the most part, law-abiding citizens. Sure, we came across a lot of folks who might have been a bit dishonest in their attempts at trying to win a monetary award from the manufacturer, but they were otherwise relatively harmless.

Such was not the case, however, in one particular situation. It seems the car manufacturer's USA headquarters in Michigan had become the victim of illegal currency manipulation. There was a man who worked in the currency department of the company whose job it was to oversee the continual exchange of marks and dollars between the company's German and American offices. Every large multinational corporation has a currency department. But what this man was really doing was playing the currency market, making the proper exchanges but often letting the money ride, producing a profit and skimming the profit for himself. He was smart and he understood the vagaries of the currency exchange market and he did well for himself.

As it happened, the man didn't work alone. He made use of overseas help. He had financial partners in Germany who basically helped launder the money as it went from dollars to marks and who set up accounts that the man could trade to and from. It was a fairly sophisticated operation and it worked well, until the man in Michigan, smart as he was, made a huge blunder one day, anticipating wrongly the direction of the currency market and accidentally losing over twenty million dollars of company money.

The loss was big enough to get noticed in an audit and the company's general counsel and secretary-treasurer, a man by the name of Ricardo, launched a full-on investigation. Ricardo suspected nefarious behavior by the currency department manager and he hired detectives who went through the man's garbage and had an entire team piece together his shredded documents. They found the evidence they were looking for and had the man arrested. It turned out that, over time, the department manager had skimmed millions from the company, not to mention the twenty million he had lost. He was found guilty in a criminal trial, but a soft judge declined to give him jail time, sentencing him instead to probation.

This is where I got involved. Ricardo called me up. He knew, of course, of my defense work on the company's product liability cases and although this was a bit of a different case, he figured I could competently handle it. Ricardo was determined to go after the man civilly. "Let's sue the bastard," he said, and that's just what we did. During the criminal case the man's partners had been revealed. We knew that they had knowledge of the millions that the man had skimmed, if not the actual whereabouts of it. By suing the department manager in civil court, we hoped, through the process of discovery, that we'd be able to find the money. Not to mention inflict, perhaps, some punitive damages on the manager.

And this is where I found out just how dangerous the man's partners were. These were no ordinary criminals. These were four very serious individuals who played hardball and weren't exactly thrilled that they'd been found out. There were warrants for their arrest but the men had gone missing. Nobody knew where they were. I had to fly to Frankfurt at one point and Ricardo made me book three different flights, picking one of the three just prior to departure.

"Ricardo," I asked, "why do I have to do that?"

"Oh, it's just routine," he assured me. "Just in case ... well, you know."

I didn't really know, but I could guess. As chief plaintiff attorney, digging into all the details for the civil trial of the Michigan malefactor, I'd become the enemy of the German guys. This was not a good position to be in. In order to stop any further investigation, these guys were willing to bring down an entire plane if they knew for sure I was on it.

Fortunately, nothing happened in Frankfurt, but back in the States, I had to travel to New York to depose a witness for the case. Ricardo traveled with me. The evening after the deposition, we were walking along a Manhattan street to dinner when I noticed two rather burly, serious-looking fellows following us. We turned down another street, and so did they. Three blocks later, I saw that they were still behind us. Then they followed us into a restaurant, taking a table next to ours, watching us the whole time.

"Ricardo," I whispered, leaning across the table, "don't look, but see the two guys sitting there?"

"Sitting where?"

"The next table. No, don't look!"

"How can I see them if I don't look?"

"Okay, go ahead and look, but don't make it obvious. These guys have been following us."

Ricardo peeked out from behind his menu and stole a glance at the next table and smiled.

"What?" I said.

"These two guys?" he said, openly pointing to them. I cringed. "Noel, these two guys are with us. I hired them for security purposes while we're here. They're two of the best." The burly men nodded curtly. Later, I honestly couldn't decide if I was more nervous when I thought the two security men might be bad guys, or if I was more nervous thinking about why we needed security guards in the first place.

At any rate, my fears dissipated two weeks later when the four German criminals were arrested in Frankfurt, at the very same airport I had flown into and out of when I'd made my trip there. They were getting ready to make their escape and were on a plane bound for Sao Paulo, Brazil. The *Bundes-grenzschutz*, the German police, somehow got tipped off and dragged the men off the plane, just as it was set to take off. In fact, the plane had been heading down the runway with the police cars in pursuit, just like in a movie. Sirens blaring and lights flashing, the police managed to get the plane stopped and then boarded the plane and arrested the men without incident. Last I heard they were all serving long sentences in Brandenburg-Görden Prison.

We ultimately settled with the ex-currency manager, but the amount was pretty small. He didn't have a lot of the money left. As for all the money that had been skimmed and sent to Germany, the German partners never revealed where it had all gone. Our civil case was trumped by the criminal proceedings and I never did get a chance to question the four bad guys, not that I have any regrets about that. To this day, millions of dollars remain missing. My understanding is that the German police managed to find a couple million in an account in Luxembourg. Who can say where the rest went? Four tough guys in Brandenburg-Görden probably know, but I'm not going to be the one who asks them.

～

The currency manipulation case was not my first brush with questionable characters. Early on, I'd represented a man suing for damages from a car accident. He'd sustained a rather unusual injury: *Dupuytren's contracture*, a condition where the fingers can no longer extend. The man claimed it happened as a result of trauma, i.e., the car accident and, in particular, his reflexive grip on the steering wheel as the accident unfolded. No other attorney would take the case. "It's not like you have an obvious case of whiplash, or a severe limp," he'd been told. But I guess I was just young enough not to know any better, so I told him I'd represent him. The thing that made the case a good one, to my mind, was that the Dupuytren's contracture had a direct bearing on the man's line of work. He was a violinist, and the injury prevented him from utilizing vibrato as he played—a technique that creates a rapidly oscillating pitch on any given note, giving the note more depth, more emotion. One uses vibrato by moving the fingers pressing on the string ever so slightly forward and back, and my client was unable to make the proper movement.

We made our case in front of the jury and apparently they were suitably impressed with it because, as I recall, the award was a fairly significant one. But that's not where the story ends. It turns out this man, unbeknownst to me, had a rather interesting past. As I was relating the details of the case over a family dinner one night, my mother-in-law interrupted.

"Wait," she said, "what did you say this man's name was?"

I told her.

"Noel," my mother-in-law said, "that man was a bank robber in Canada!"

"What? How do you know that?"

Turns out that my mother-in-law's deceased husband Jack, a man I'd never gotten the chance to meet, had done some charity work from time to time in a prison, talking with the inmates and offering counseling. One day he met a certain violinist who was incarcerated in the prison who had quite a tale to tell. On a whim, he'd stolen a plane at a small municipal airport close to Detroit and had taken off on a joyride. The problem was, he wasn't a pilot. Somewhere along the line, he'd received a little flying experience but he wasn't particularly keen on actually doing what was legally necessary to get a pilot's license. And not only was he not a pilot, he apparently wasn't much of a navigator, either. After a couple hours of flying that day, he'd gotten himself lost, landing eventually in Canada.

Then, as if he hadn't already exercised enough poor judgment, he elected to do something more stupid yet. Figuring he had nothing to lose in Canada, he decided to walk into a small bank and rob it. He didn't get far with his take, however, before the Royal Canadian Mounted Police—who, they say, always get their man—got him. I don't know what became of the robbery charges, but he was subsequently extradited to the U.S. where he was tried and found guilty of grand theft of a private plane and sentenced to prison where my mother-in-law's husband met him.

Now, I guess that since the arrest and extradition took place in Canada, the man's background was left undiscovered by the opposing defense team in our case. My research was usually more thorough and I like to think that if I had been the defense attorney, I'd have found out about the man's past. Since he was my client, it never occurred to me to dig too extensively. But had the defense brought up the man's felonies and prison time, I can't imagine we'd have won the case.

To my knowledge, the man was never in trouble with the law again, electing to straighten up and fly right, so to speak. He took the award from the case, had some major surgery on his hands, and continued his musical career. Once he invited me to the club where he played with a string quartet, and I watched him as he played the violin with skill and dexterity and a beautiful vibrato.

⌐

Some characters are more questionable than others. I once represented a man who was a member of a certain "family," let us say. The man couldn't pay me his legal bill. I didn't know of his connections when I took his case. But his connections became apparent when he offered to make payment in the form of trade, giving me for free a service he typically reserved for his employers.

"Listen, Noel," he said, "I'll make you a deal. You ever need any help with a problem client, maybe someone's giving you a hard time, you get a hold of me and I'll take care of them."

"Take care of them?"

"Yeah, you know. Take care of 'em."

"You mean like ...."

"Put 'em in cement shoes. It's what I do," he shrugged.

"Thanks, I'll ... I'll try to remember that."

"Sure. Anytime."

About a year later, the man called me out of the blue. It seems his employers weren't paying him what had been promised.

"I wanna sue," he said. Obviously, I didn't want to sue his employers, knowing who they were, but I didn't want to tell the man no, either. He didn't exactly seem like the type who would take no for an answer. So we sued, with me hoping for some kind of quick settlement so that I could get the hell out from between these two particular parties.

Two days after the employer was served, I got a call from the client. "Noel," he said, "don't worry about the case going to court."

"You mean they called you and settled?" I was feeling relieved.

"Well, not exactly. We're going to mediation. It's all set."

"Mediation? But I haven't been informed of that. How can it be all set? I haven't requested a mediation."

"Well, it's not exactly what you'd call a *formal* mediation."

"No?"

"No. It's more like a family mediation. We're gonna get together and talk things out. At the Holiday Inn. And I want you there."

What could I do? For good or for bad, I had a duty to represent my client. We went to the Holiday Inn. I didn't feel like taking any chances, though. I happened to have a concealed weapons permit and I made use of it, tucking a small handgun into a holster beneath my suit jacket.

When we got to the Holiday Inn, we knocked on the door of the room that we'd been informed was to be the "mediation" room. A very large man with a thick neck and wearing a suit that he seemed to be bursting out of opened the door, stepped outside, and closed it behind him.

"You can go in," the large man said to my client. Then looking at me, he said, "You can't."

"But I'm his attorney. He's my client."

"I understand. But this is strictly ... a family matter."

"Noel," said my client. "It's okay. Why don't you go down to the coffee shop and wait for me."

"Are you sure?"

"Sure I'm sure."

I stood for a moment or two while the very large man eyed me suspiciously and then I turned and began walking down the hallway.

"By the way," I heard the man say behind me. I turned and he pointed at me. "I know what's underneath your suit jacket." I turned again and kept walking, a bit faster this time.

Down in the coffee shop I waited. And waited. An hour went by. Then two. Where was my client? I didn't know for sure if he was still even in the room where I'd left him. Maybe they'd all gone "for a ride," as the saying goes and I would never see him again.

Finally he walked into the coffee shop.

"Well, the case is all settled," he grinned.

"It is? How?"

"It's all settled, Noel. That's what's important."

"Yeah, but —."

"Noel. Believe me. You don't want to know."

And I guess I really didn't. Like the whereabouts of the money in the currency manipulation case, some things are probably best left as mysteries. This time the man paid me, and with a check instead of an offer for free services. I never heard from him again, which was fine by me. The case was a success. The parties had settled. Like the man said, that's what's important.

CHAPTER FIVE
The Best Three Days

IN MY PRIME I WAS a tenacious lawyer and known to go to any and all lengths to win a case. But what I ended up doing back in 1965 for my friend Marty Benson was extreme even by my standards.

Marty owned a Beechcraft V-tailed Bonanza airplane which he flew regularly. He entrusted the maintenance of the plane to a company that specialized in servicing all manner of aircraft, including Marty's Bonanza. They would do routine and preventive maintenance, and (ostensibly) make certain that the airplane was always fit to fly. One day, Marty was flying about 8,000 feet above Memphis, Tennessee, when the cabin of his plane suddenly started filling with smoke. Marty couldn't see a thing and after radioing in a distress call, he was immediately cleared to land at a small municipal airport close by. An excellent pilot, Marty, with limited vision and a cockpit filled with smoke, somehow, miraculously, landed the plane safely. He came out of it without so much as a scratch.

Now, when the FAA investigated the incident, as they do for every airplane mishap, they determined that an oil gasket had been improperly installed during the plane's most recent servicing, thus leading ultimately to the situation Marty found himself in above Memphis. Marty approached the company, let us say, in a less-than-cordial mood. He'd almost been killed, after all. A lesser pilot probably would have been.

And so when he demanded the company give him a new engine to replace the one that had been rendered inoperable by the company's own incompetence, he felt the request was more than reasonable.

The company thought otherwise.

"Well, let's see," a company representative told him, "your engine had 800 hours on it. Now, the life of that engine is only about 1400 hours. That means you only had roughly forty percent of the engine life remaining. So, how about we give you a rebuilt engine and we'll compensate you to the tune of forty percent of the cost? That's the best we can do."

Well, their best was unacceptable to Marty and that's when he came to me.

"Marty," I said, "I understand your frustration, but it's not really all that much money. I'm not sure it's worth a lawsuit. The time and expense. Sure, we can probably show liability, but by the time the case would go to court ...."

"There must be something you can do, Noel," Marty pleaded. "I mean those bastards almost had me killed."

"Yeah, I can imagine it must have been pretty scary."

"Scary?" said Marty. "I had diarrhea for three days!"

And that's when it hit me. We didn't just have a product liability case. We had a personal injury case.

"Okay, Marty," I said. "Let's sue the bastards."

At a pretrial motion I was approached by the company's attorney. They'd hired one of the biggest law firms in the state.

"Hey, kid," the attorney said. "Why don't you take my advice and drop this suit?"

"Drop the suit? Why would I do that?"

"'Cause you can't win it. There's just no way."

"And why is that?"

"I'll tell you why. Because you don't know how to fly a

goddamn airplane. That's why. Here. Take my card. Call me if you want to settle. Maybe I can get the company to split the cost of a rebuilt engine for your guy or something. I can at least try to do that so you don't come away completely empty-handed."

I was young and I knew the other attorney was just trying to intimidate me, but I couldn't get what he said out of my mind. Deep down I knew he was right. What did I really know about airplanes? Did I have the necessary expertise to get across to a jury exactly what my client went through, the mechanics of it, the difficulty in landing, the miraculous nature of what Marty had done? I needed to paint a picture for the jury and that meant learning all the intricacies of flight. Little by little I began to consider that there was only one way I could properly represent Marty. I had to learn to fly.

Now it turns out that the airplane servicing company also had a flight school. What better way to learn, I reasoned, than at the hands of the very guys we were suing? I could speak to the jury from a position of expertise—expertise the defense would find difficult to contest since it would be acquired from them. So the very next weekend, I signed up. Naturally I didn't bother to tell them I was an attorney bent on suing their company.

"What kind of plane do I learn on?" I asked the guy in charge of the school. A low-wing Cherokee, he told me. That, of course, wouldn't do. I needed to know what it was like to fly the plane Marty was almost killed in.

"Hmm," I said, "that's okay, I suppose, but I'm really interested in learning in a Beechcraft Bonanza."

"Well, that's a fast plane," the instructor said, "with a whole slew of different features. We prefer to start our students with the Cherokee."

"I see," I said, and then thinking quickly, added, "Well, it's too bad because I really wanted to learn how to fly the plane I'm going to buy." The servicing company also sold planes and the instructor recognized an opportunity when he saw one. I was not just a student; I was a potential customer.

"Of course, Mr. Gage, we can certainly make an exception for you."

And so I learned how to fly a Beechcraft Bonanza. Over the course of the next several weeks, I took all the classes and did all the necessary coursework and sat behind the controls as the instructor taught me the ins and outs. And I managed to accomplish it all before the case came to trial. The lead instructor and some of the guys from the school were in attendance on the first day of the trial and the look on their faces when I walked in was priceless.

"Noel," they said, "what are *you* doing here?"

"Me? Oh, I'm the attorney for the plaintiff."

The trial got underway and my flight training made it possible for me to properly question the company's representatives and put together a killer closing summation. I talked about glide patterns and pitch and trim and calculated air speed and lateral stability and all sorts of things the defendants had taught me. Our side looked more expert than their side. The defendant's attorney, who seemed so intimidating to me before, now seemed intimidated himself. He kept shifting uncomfortably in his chair. And of course, I didn't leave out the emotional factor. I talked about the three days of diarrhea and I also talked about the schoolyard full of kids next to the airport that we were all grateful Marty had managed to avoid crashing into.

For good measure, I brought in a doctor to testify. Gerald Weingarden was, and still is, a practicing physician in West

Palm Beach, Florida. He specializes in aviation medicine and performs medical exams for the FAA. By so doing, he makes our skies safer. Jerry's a great guy and a good friend. Tall and good-looking and affable, the jury loved him. He not only testified about the diarrhea, but also about something else Marty suffered from as a result of the traumatic experience: urticaria. "A very serious case of urticaria," he said on the stand. Now, urticaria is a fancy word for hives but the jury didn't know that and the defense attorney didn't bother to ask. Urticaria sounds a lot scarier than hives and so that's what we called it.

The jury didn't deliberate very long before awarding Marty a rebuilt engine and an additional $60,000. This was 1963. Today, based on inflation, that award would come to almost half a million bucks. "Best three days of diarrhea I ever spent," said Marty.

As for me, after flight school, I never flew a plane again. I was an hour of instruction away from securing my license and, truthfully, I'm glad I never got around to getting it. I wouldn't have flown enough to stay sharp. People who don't fly regularly probably shouldn't fly at all.

And there was something of a little mishap on my final cross-country flight test. I flew one leg of the flight with my instructor, and then, getting ready to take off for the next leg, I went to check the fuel, per standard operating procedure.

"Forget it," the instructor said. "We have plenty, I'm sure."

"Yeah, but if I've learned one thing in training, it's—."

"I said forget it. Besides, we have a little weather coming in. Let's get going."

It's probably not too hard to guess what happened. The story ends in the cornfield of an irate farmer. When the engine started sputtering, I turned the controls over to the instructor.

"You got us into this mess," I said. "You get us out."

He glided us down no worse for wear but took out a sizable amount of the farmer's corn in the process. Once the farmer stopped shouting obscenities at us, I promised to pay for the corn and made one final request: "Can we buy some gas from you?"

Meanwhile, the best part of the trial against the maintenance company came twenty-one days after the award. I knew that the defendants had twenty days to file an appeal. On the twenty-first day, with no appeal coming, and wanting to make sure we'd collect, I showed up at the company's building with the sheriff and a writ of execution. From a phone booth outside, I called the company's attorney to let him know we were there to collect, one way or the other. Either a check or, as I told him, a nice new Bonanza of theirs that I had my eye on. They could take their choice.

"Neither," the attorney sneered. "I'm filing an appeal right now!"

"Better count the days since the trial," I said. "I think you might be just one day too late."

After a long pause, I heard him mumble, "I'll be right down there."

A little later he showed up red-faced and clearly angry with himself, and carrying a personal check good for the amount of the jury award. It seemed he was so embarrassed to have failed his client by missing the appeal deadline that he had offered to pay the entire award out of his own pocket. I managed to somehow keep my satisfaction to myself. Sure, he was experienced and I was still young and learning, but you don't have to be the world's greatest attorney to be able to properly read a calendar. Chalk one up for the kid.

Now, it was worth it to me, of course, to have learned to fly as part of my trial strategy. We won and we won big and Marty and I were both happy. But a year or so later, I was compelled to wonder at the cost of representing Marty. It ended up being more than just having to go through flight school. For as it turns out, Marty wasn't exactly alone that fateful day when his cabin filled with smoke above Memphis. A rather attractive blonde was on board with him, an attractive blonde who happened to be Marty's secretary and not his wife. Marty was successful at keeping his passenger a secret during the FAA investigation, but eventually word somehow got back to his wife. The next time I represented Marty, it was in his divorce.

We did pretty well in divorce court, all things considered; but, as they say, hell hath no fury. As it happens, Marty's wife went on to marry the second-in-command at the Internal Revenue Service. He stayed in his position for fifteen years. And for fifteen years, each and every year, like clockwork, there was one thing Marty and I could always count on: an IRS audit. It never failed. Just another cost of representing Marty, I guess. But I much preferred the first case; not surprisingly, learning to fly is a lot more fun than getting audited by the IRS every year. Hell, root canal would be more fun. Come to think of it, given a choice, I believe I'd even take three days of diarrhea.

CHAPTER SIX

M. D.

DURING MY TIME IN Detroit, trying the product liability cases, my personal life was undergoing more alterations than the junkyard auto with two VIN numbers. Hilda and I had had three children, a boy and two girls. Hilda had started out as a teacher, but my career had produced in her a keen interest in the law and she gave up her career in education and became a lawyer. Eventually, she'd serve as a judge in the circuit court. But in time, Hilda and I divorced.

Subsequently, returning to the office one time after having been out of town for a few days for a deposition, I noticed a new intern that Marty Doctoroff had hired. "Who's the new girl?" I asked. Her name was Ivy, and before long Ivy and I were dating. Ultimately, we married and with Ivy, I'd be blessed with three more daughters.

My firm kept working for the car manufacturer, but there were other product liability cases, too. Like the Case of the Tomato Dust. This one took place before Judge "Tiger" Thornton. Tiger was in his mid-eighties and had served seemingly forever. In fact, he'd been appointed by President Harry Truman. And Tiger had no intention of stepping down from the bench anytime soon. Not that there was any reason for him to. He was popular, well-respected, and mentally agile. He hadn't slowed down a bit.

Tiger had a sharp sense of humor to boot. We had all heard about the time a criminal defendant, explaining his actions, had said to him, "The Lord told me to do it." Tiger had turned to the prosecutor, asking, "Are you sure you've indicted the right defendant?"

I'd been in front of Judge Thornton a couple of times before the Tomato Dust Case and had witnessed his sense of humor personally. During one case, he had called the opposing counsel and me into his chambers to apologize that the trial had been delayed a week due to, of all things, Tiger's honeymoon. Seems he'd just gotten married, and to a much younger woman. He was eighty-two at the time. Naturally we congratulated the old man.

"And let me tell you both something," he said. "You young fellows probably can't appreciate an old guy like me getting married, but I'm here to say that the honeymoon was incredible. You might not believe it, but I had sex almost every night!"

The other counsel and I exchanged glances, wondering at the disclosure of such personal information, but then we both cracked up when he continued:

"Almost on Monday night, almost on Tuesday night, almost on Wednesday night ...."

In the Tomato Dust Case, we represented a major chemical manufacturer from California who sold a product for dusting tomatoes to keep the bugs away. It was a common enough product and for forty years they'd sold it without incident, tens of millions of dollars' worth. But one day in Detroit, a woman used the dust on tomato plants in her backyard garden and very shortly afterwards, fell over, comatose. Her sister was present and rushed her to the hospital where she was ultimately diagnosed with a rare, life-threatening dermatological condition known as Stevens-Johnson syndrome, a form of toxic epidermal necrolysis where cell death causes the epidermis to separate from the dermis. In short, the outer layer of her skin was peeling away in patches.

Before the woman had been afflicted, she'd been a beautiful African-American who looked as though she'd stepped off the pages of *Ebony* magazine. As a result of the syndrome, she'd been rendered blind, her skin was denuded resulting in stark black and white patches, her fingernails and toenails had fallen off, and she'd spent months in intensive care. Her attorney, a friend of mine and a high-caliber plaintiff's lawyer, argued, as had been the determination of the hospital staff, that the syndrome had been caused by the use of the tomato dust which the woman had unwittingly inhaled. It was the only connection they could seem to make.

I knew I needed an expert to counter the claims of the plaintiff but I had no idea what kind of expert to get. This was beyond the expertise of your typical general physician. Eventually, I settled on two experts, a dermatologist and an allergist. I knew the cause of the woman's affliction could not have been my client's chemical. Even though the plaintiffs had made a connection, there was nothing in its forty-year history to indicate such a consequence of using the product. Both of my experts, coming at the problem from their own respective disciplines, would be able to offer testimony that something else must have been behind the woman's reaction.

The problem was that the experts didn't come cheap. The dermatologist wanted $60,000, a hefty sum in the late 1970s when the trial took place. Because we were working under a West Coast law firm who had hired us on behalf of the company, as the case was in Michigan, I called the managing partner of the firm, tentatively explaining my need for the expense.

"Pay it!" he said. "We don't care what you spend. Just win the case. The client is facing millions in damages not to mention the destruction of a profitable product line, one they've banked on for years." And then he repeated: *Just win the case.*

The dermatologist was worth the fee. He oozed both authority and credibility. I questioned him on the stand and could tell the jury was riveted. He talked slowly and understandably and made eye contact with the jurors throughout his testimony. It was almost as if he was gently teaching them. Based on my discovery, he had looked closely at the woman's background and had learned about her trips to a dermatologist prior to her use of the tomato dust. Towards the end of my questioning I asked him if there was anything further he needed to render his opinion as to the true source of the plaintiff's affliction.

"Well, yes, Mr. Gage. I've not yet had the chance to examine this lady personally. With the court's permission, I'd like to do that now. I think it would prove very helpful with respect to determining the real truth of this matter."

"Please proceed," said Judge Tiger Thornton. The dermatologist stepped down from the stand and walked over to where the plaintiff was seated. Very gently, very professionally, very patiently, he inspected her skin and scalp and examined her nails, thanking her all the while for her cooperation. His bedside manner was impeccable. At long last he returned to the stand.

"I'm quite ready to present to you my considered opinion, Mr. Gage," he said.

"Please do," I said.

"Based on my expertise and experience spanning over thirty years, I'm quite comfortable concluding that this woman's Stevens-Johnson syndrome was not caused by a reaction to the chemical in the tomato dust. Instead, it's my considered opinion that her unfortunate state of affairs was caused by the dapsone treatment her dermatologist had given her."

Dapsone. We had discovered that the woman had been treated by her dermatologist for pustular psoriasis and the dermatologist had used dapsone, an anti-infective agent licensed at the time only for the use of treating, of all things, leprosy. It's pretty serious stuff and it had been applied to her by her dermatologist just a week or so before she presented with Stevens-Johnson symptoms. Why he'd used it was anybody's guess, but the woman had no doubt had a severe reaction to it and such a reaction was not unprecedented. Stevens-Johnson Syndrome, though exceedingly rare, was a known side effect of dapsone. The connection seemed clear enough.

The allergist confirmed the findings of our dermatologist. Not taking any chances and remembering the managing partner's words to me (*just win the case*) I even had a third expert physician testify from California. Unfortunately, an illness prevented him from making the trip for the trial but in the days before video, he at least was able to provide deposition testimony. The question was how best to present that testimony to the jury. Should I just read it to them? Would that be effective? After some lengthy consideration, I decided to have the physician's testimony read to the jury, but not by me: by an actor. I went to the Detroit Institute of Arts and held auditions, settling on a handsome older man who looked to me like he could pass for a trusted, old-fashioned family doctor. Naturally I explained to the jury that the witness was merely reading the words of the real doctor—Dr. Spencer— but by the time the actor had finished with his convincing recitation of Dr. Spencer's testimony, that little piece of information had been forgotten by jury and judge alike.

"Careful stepping down, Doctor Spencer," Tiger Thornton said. "There's a step."

Between the $60,000 dermatologist and the adept actor,

we won the case. The tragic thing was that the misbegotten pursuit of our client had cost valuable time. The woman's dermatologist was certainly culpable. But by the end of our trial, the statute of limitations had expired, and no further action could be taken against that malefactor.

⌒

The Tomato Dust Case made me realize something. I could be a much better, and more valuable, attorney if I knew more about the medical field. I was getting into bigger cases with bigger injuries and more serious, sometimes complex, medical conditions. It would help if I was something of an expert myself. And so I set out to know more. But not just a little more. I decided I was going to get a medical degree. I was going to become an M.D.

I've always had a great deal of respect for doctors. Some, like Gerald Weingarden, have been crucial to my work and have also become good friends. Ralph Cash was another. Ralph was an outstanding pediatrician and I can never forget the story he told me once about the woman who called him in the middle of the night asking for advice.

"I just had sex with a man," she said, "and I'm afraid I might get pregnant. It would just kill my husband. What can I do?"

"Lady, I'm a pediatrician. Why are you calling me?"

"Well, you're a doctor, right? You work with kids? So you must know how to prevent them. I mean, even after sex, right?"

"Sure. Here's what you do. Stand on your head with your feet up against the wall for half an hour." Then Ralph hung up. I imagine the woman probably took his advice.

Ralph had a couple of exceptionally talented kids.

Howard Cash is a renowned expert in DNA analysis and was called upon to identify all the victims of 9/11. Sandy Cash moved to Israel and has become a very accomplished folk singer.

When I made the decision to earn an M.D., I naturally assumed I'd be able to enroll in a local medical school. But I quickly learned that without a pre-med degree, I wasn't going to be accepted anywhere. I had one lonely class in zoology during my undergraduate years and that didn't exactly qualify. And so I expanded my search and after a lot of looking, I found two schools that would admit me. But one was on the Caribbean island of Montserrat and the other was on Grenada, both way too far to commute. So I kept looking. Finally, after weeks of searching, I came across a school in the states that would take me: Spartan Health Sciences in El Paso, Texas. I flew down there in 1981 and enrolled—over the objections of a very skeptical dean.

"Mr. Gage, I think you're wasting your time and your money," he said. "You have no pre-med. That's going to make it damn near impossible for you."

"I'll just have to study harder."

"And you're considering commuting a couple times a week? All the way from Detroit?"

"I'll fly down regularly."

"Frankly, I don't see how you're going to be able to pull it off."

"Let me try," I implored. "If I make it, will you let me stay and graduate?"

The dean reluctantly agreed and wished me luck. And I did well. It was tiring and at times overwhelming but I was learning the material and passing the exams. A year and a half later, however, the dean was replaced. I was called into the new dean's office.

"Doctor Gage," he began, as it was customary to call the students "doctor" even before graduation, "I think we have a problem. I see that you are not maintaining our required eighty-five percent attendance requirement."

"Well, no, not exactly. I'm running a law firm in Detroit, you know. But I get down here once or twice a week and as you can see by my grades, I'm doing very well."

"Yes, but the attendance requirement is quite clear. All students have to maintain an eighty-five percent attendance rate."

"Of course. But, you see, I had an unofficial agreement with your predecessor. If I could make the grades, I could graduate, notwithstanding my level of attendance. "

"I don't really care what the old dean did or did not agree to, Doctor Gage. If we make an exception for you, where would it stop?"

"But I've been proceeding under the assumption that the dean spoke for the university." I couldn't help it; I dug into my legal training and continued: "Have you, sir, ever heard of the legal concept of 'detrimental reliance'?"

The approach didn't go over well. "I don't care to hear your lawyer crap, Doctor Gage. There are no exceptions to the rule. All students must maintain eighty-five percent attendance. It's really quite clear and I have no interest in discussing the matter. You simply cannot graduate if you cannot attend."

I left the dean's office completely dejected. A year and a half of commuting between Detroit and El Paso was down the drain. I must have logged close to a million miles in the air and it was all coming to nothing. Then, walking down the hallway towards the exit, I saw it. A godsend disguised as a help-wanted poster: *Wanted – Qualified Person with Legal Background to Teach Medical Law Class.* The rule, as the dean duly noted, was that all *students* must maintain attendance. I applied for the teaching position and was soon no longer just a student. I was a bona-fide faculty member and it seemed faculty members were afforded exceptions to student rules. I stayed and completed my coursework.

The only other potential problem was my rotations. But it wasn't a problem with the school; they allowed me to fulfill my rotation requirements at a Michigan hospital. The problem was with the hospital, or, in particular, the senior resident of the hospital who called me in one day and insisted that I take a night shift rotation for an entire week. Unlike the other students doing their rotations, I was older, of course, and with another full-time occupation; namely, a thriving law practice. I didn't mind doing the work, but I drew the line at pulling a night shift, and I told him so.

"Then I'm afraid we're going to have a problem," he said. "If you're unwilling to take a night rotation, I'm not going to be able to allow you to pass your rotations requirement."

Fortunately, I happened to have an ace up my sleeve.

"I'm not sure forcing me to take a night rotation would be such a great idea," I said.

"And why not?"

"Because if I start doing night shifts, I'm going to be awfully tired in the mornings."

"Yes. So?"

"It just so happens that my law firm is currently engaged by this hospital's administrator in a malpractice suit. If I go into my law office every morning wiped out from being here all night, I imagine it's going to be hard for me to do the best job I can do for the administrator, thus risking having him lose the suit, exposing him to the possibility of having to pay out tens of thousands of dollars. And if he should ask why we lost the case, I'd feel compelled to be completely honest with him, telling him that I was not at my best because the senior resident forced me to work nights during the duration of the case. And I would really hate to have to put you in such an awkward position."

"Well," the senior resident said, thinking the matter over, "I suppose, given these ... unique circumstances that ... this one time ... yes, I think we can waive the night rotation for you."

"Splendid," I smiled. "I was hoping you'd see it that way."

I graduated soon after. I was now Noel Gage, J.D., M.D.

CHAPTER SEVEN

My Introduction to the Finer Things

AS A TRIAL LAWYER, you find yourself in front of judges quite often, of course. But judges are citizens, too, and even they need legal representation from time to time. One day, I received a call from the chief judge of the 36th District Court in Detroit, the largest district court in the state. The judge asked if I'd heard about the problem with the court building. I had. It had been all over the news. The building that housed the court was leased from the city. The building was old, a converted department store warehouse. That judge and more than a hundred other people working at the building had to be evacuated by stretcher one day after being exposed to unidentified toxic fumes. At least seventy people were taken to nearby hospitals. The judge was understandably shaken by the incident and wanted the city of Detroit to answer for the hazardous condition of the building.

I ended up with over a hundred clients—judges, court personnel, citizens—who happened to be in the building that day. I brought in experts and it was determined that the building's air intake vents were outdated and located in areas that were especially susceptible to exhaust fumes from the heavy automobile traffic outside the building. Coupled with the hot, hazy, still weather conditions of the day in question, it became a perfect storm of sorts that the building's ventilation system simply wasn't capable of handling.

Meanwhile, because of the incident, multiple workers'

compensation claims and other medical claims had been paid, totaling in the hundreds of thousands of dollars. I was contacted by the Michigan Supreme Court. The Court, quite justifiably, wanted restitution from the city. They retained my services and to my knowledge I became the only lawyer the Supreme Court ever hired on a contingent fee basis.

Now, with so many potential plaintiffs, I could have proceeded on a class action basis. The problem with class action suits, however, is that the presiding judge is much more involved in how the case gets presented by the plaintiff (even appointing the attorney, though the appointment routinely goes to the lawyer who filed the suit), as well as how much the damages should be and how the damages are to be distributed. And so I decided instead to sue on behalf of each individual. But I did so collectively. That way, I only needed to file once rather than file more than a hundred times (each time with its own respective filing fee). But more important, I knew the city had a much better chance of defending itself against one plaintiff at a time. If the plaintiff, for example, could be shown to have had some medical condition—maybe a heart condition, or even just a bad cold on the day of the fumes—the city could have claimed that it was the medical condition that overcame the plaintiff and not any alleged toxicity from poor ventilation. Throw a hundred plaintiffs at them at once, however, and it becomes nearly impossible to explain them all away. It was a natural foil to the Union Picnic case.

The city knew what it was up against. The trial was set to begin not in a courtroom but, because of the sheer number of people involved, in an auditorium. It would have been quite a spectacle and media circus. The city wisely settled before the trial even got started and I was able to secure a sizable amount for everybody involved.

The nice thing is that the judges I represented, legal experts though they were, were nevertheless comfortable in letting me run the show on their behalf. It was a gratifying win and even though the paperwork was monumental because of the number of plaintiffs, I was able, in one fell swoop, to add more than a hundred people to the firm's clientele. Not bad for a single case.

⌒

For the most part, I was still representing the car manufacturer; however, I represented a car dealer, too. Tom Sullivan ran a thriving dealership in Southfield, a suburb of Detroit, and one day Tom came to me in a state of agitation.

"Noel," he said, "isn't this America?"

"What do you mean, Tom?" I said, taken aback by the seemingly random nature of the question.

Tom had a very deliberate way of speaking that revealed a thoughtful kind of intelligence, which served him well in the business world. His dealership was one of the most profitable ones in the state.

"I *mean*," he added slowly, "isn't this still the United States of America?"

"Well, of course this is still the United States of America," I replied.

"Then why won't they let me open my dealership on a Saturday?"

"What? Why won't *who* let you open your dealership?"

"The union." Aha. Seems Tom's sales staff had organized, becoming part of a prominent Detroit-based union. It was happening seemingly everywhere and now it was happening at Tom's dealership. "Can you help me, Noel?" Tom continued. "Because I plan on being open this Saturday and I have a feeling that that might create a problem or two with the union."

"Sure, Tom. I'll see what I can do."

I liked Tom and Tom had come to trust me. He had come to me originally when the best friend and roommate of his daughter had gotten into trouble in school. They'd been attending Western Michigan University in Kalamazoo together. One night the roommate-friend had apparently gone to the wrong party. Some kids had been smoking marijuana in a back bedroom and the party had gotten busted. The police arrested everyone in attendance and the girl had called Tom's daughter in hysterics. Tom's daughter had called Tom and Tom, in turn, had called me.

"Can you get my daughter's friend out of this jam?" he said. It was midnight but I said sure, and I immediately drove the two hours to Kalamazoo where I not only got her out, but I got the charges dropped. Tom was my loyal client from that point on.

Regarding his current case, I knew what the union was capable of. Back in those days it was a kind of rough and tumble group that wasn't above sending a few thugs somewhere to get a message across. Tom was playing with fire to open his store expressly against the rules of the union. They didn't take kindly to being crossed. But Tom was right. It *was* America and it seemed to me he had a right to open on Saturday, an otherwise pretty big sales day in the automobile industry. I needed to find a way to help.

Now it so happened that I'd also been representing the Southfield Police Officers Association in legal matters. That relationship would come in handy more than a few times. For Tom, I called in a favor, getting a couple of plainclothes cops to patrol the parking lot of the dealership that Saturday and a couple of firemen up on the roof with fire hoses. In addition, I hired a photographer to stand by. Sure enough, mid-afternoon, no fewer than twenty union thugs showed up.

The thugs sauntered around the parking lot making their presence known. The plainclothes cops perked up, keeping a close watch. Of course the union guys weren't necessarily doing anything illegal yet. But legitimate customers floating around the dealership looking at Tom's inventory were becoming decidedly uncomfortable. There were a lot of them, what with Tom's dealership the only one opened that day. His was a popular dealership anyway, clean and spotless. The service area sparkled and Tom made sure all the employees were friendly and helpful. But now the thugs had more or less taken over the place and the customers began to leave. They sensed what the cops sensed; things were about to get ugly.

Before long, the thugs formed a circle in the lot, obscuring, so they thought, a couple of guys in the middle of the circle who commenced to hurl bricks through the store's plate glass windows. The photographer managed to snap a couple of good shots of them and then the firemen, unseen until then, let loose with the hoses. Naturally that dispersed the group in a hurry. The police officers arrested the two who'd thrown the bricks and took them in. With the photographs of the brick-tossing pair in action, it was going to be a pretty easy case for the police. My hope was that we'd sent a strong message that Tom was willing to fight fire with fire. He wasn't about to back down.

Shortly after the thugs had been booked, I received a phone call in my office. It was none other than the head of the union. "Gage," he demanded, "I want my boys released within the next hour."

"Well, I'm afraid that's not my function, sir. It's a police matter at this point."

"I don't give a damn what your function is, Gage. You've embarrassed my union and you've got sixty minutes to get my boys out."

"Well, I can't speak for the city, sir. I'm just a lawyer. My influence extends only so far and —."

"I know better than that, Gage. I've done my homework. I know you represent those guys and I know they'll listen to you. Besides, I don't happen to think your client Mr. Sullivan wants to press charges anyway."

"No? And why would that be?"

"Because of the deal I'm ready to make."

"Deal?"

"Yeah. Listen, Gage, you get my guys out within one hour and from now on, your client's dealership will not only be open on Saturdays, it'll be the only one open on Saturdays in the whole state of Michigan. What do you think of that?"

It was a deal I could not refuse. "I'll see what I can do."

"The deal's off the table in sixty minutes, Gage."

"I understand." I then made a few well-placed phone calls and exactly fifty-nine minutes later, the thugs walked out. The union leader kept his word. The union could be threatening and the members could be bullies, but there was a certain code of honor when it came to keeping one's word back then. The union would exert its influence on the employees of other car dealerships around the state, but Tom's dealership was open for business every Saturday from that point on and he benefited enormously.

Tom was so grateful that he asked me if I'd like to come along with him on a trip to Las Vegas. I said sure, why not. I'd never been to Las Vegas and the trip was entertaining from the start. We flew first class on a TWA jet and Tom, close to sixty, thin, and with light hair, just happened to bear a remarkable resemblance to Howard Hughes. He even had longish fingernails just like the famous recluse and owner of the airline we were on.

Shortly after takeoff one of the stewardesses leaned down and whispered in my ear, "Is that who I think it is?"

I couldn't resist. "Yes, but please keep it to yourself. Mr. Hughes isn't comfortable with a lot of fuss. He prefers his anonymity. You understand, I'm sure."

"Of course!" she said. "Your secret is safe with me." But then I watched as she whispered one by one to the other stewardesses, all of whom couldn't stop peeking over at us as they made their way up and down the aisle. And for the rest of that flight, we received more attention and more free food and drink than I have ever received on a plane before or since.

"They sure are friendly," Tom said at one point and I felt compelled to confess as to just why that was. Tom laughed and felt by then it was better not to correct the impression. "It would break their hearts," he said. I have no doubt that for years afterwards every member of that flight crew told the story of the day they served Howard Hughes in his first-class seat.

We stayed at the Sands Hotel in a two-bedroom suite with an oversized living room and had dinner the first night in the Regency Room, their five-star restaurant. Still not a drinker at the time, I ordered a Coke. Tom ordered a bottle of something called Chateau Lafite Rothschild upon which I noticed a marked change in the pallor of the waiter. Noticing things like that was something I'd become proficient in as a trial attorney. I couldn't imagine what the problem was, but something certainly had the waiter disconcerted.

"I'm afraid I'll have to check with the maître d, sir," the waiter said. Then he trotted off and half a minute later the maître d came over.

"I'm sorry, sir," the maître d said. "I'm afraid we're not going to be able to accommodate your request for the Chateau Lafite Rothschild." At this, the lawyer in me came out. Tom was my client, after all.

"Let me see the manager," I demanded. The maître d excused himself and returned shortly with the manager of the restaurant who explained to us with a somewhat nervous smile that it was the restaurant's position to not, as a matter of course, provide the more expensive wines to guests who were being comped by the hotel, which the waiter, maître d, and manager had all assumed was the case with Tom.

"*Senator* Sullivan," I said, with what I thought was appropriate hyperbole for the situation, "is perfectly capable of paying for your wine. We don't need nor expect to be comped for anything. Now, please bring the man a bottle of what he'd requested."

"Yes sir!"

"And while you're at it, bring me one, too!" The waiter and maître d and manager all scurried off and within moments, two bottles of wine arrived at our table.

"I can't drink them both, Noel," Tom laughed. "I'm afraid you'll have to drink the second. You ordered it after all." It was my first time drinking and the wine tasted acceptable to me although of course I had nothing in my experience to compare it to.

"It's good, Tom," I said somewhere in the middle of my second glass. "Nice flavor. Hearty bouquet." Phrases I had heard in movies and television commercials. "What's it called again?"

"Chateau Lafite Rothschild," Tom smiled.

"Hmm. And just how expensive *is* this wine?"

"This wine? Fifteen-hundred dollars a bottle."

Now it was my turn to have my pallor change. I imagine I went completely white, followed by the red of pure embarrassment. "What?! Cripes, Tom. I would never have ordered —."

Tom just laughed. "Relax," he said. "Thanks to you I made more money than that just this past Saturday."

I drink wine to this day. Hell of a way to be introduced to it. The funny thing is about a month later a gentleman stopped by the office who needed representation in a legal matter he'd become embroiled in. But seeing our fee schedule, he said he'd have to look elsewhere. Unfortunately, he explained, we were just a bit beyond his budget.

"I'm sorry," I said. Then I thought for a moment. "Hey, wait a second," I said as he moved towards the door. "What did you say the name of your company is?"

"L & L Wine. Why do you ask?"

"Do you happen to have any Chateau Lafite Rothschild?"

"Sure. We've got four cases in our warehouse."

"Mister," I smiled, "you've got yourself a lawyer."

CHAPTER EIGHT

My Friend the Police Chief

DURING MY TIME representing the Southfield Police Officers Association I got to know the captain of the department fairly well. Ed Ritenour was a great guy and a great cop. Eventually he'd become Chief of Police and years later, after his retirement, he'd become a private investigator. We remained friends throughout.

The Southfield Police Department grew immensely during Ed's thirty years there. Southfield was just a township in 1955 when Ed came aboard the department and Ed was just the fifth cop the township hired. By his third year he'd worked his way up to Detective-Sergeant. By his thirtieth, there were a hundred and eighty men on the force working under him and Southfield had turned into high-rises and freeways.

Ed and I often got together and swapped war stories, mine revolving around some interesting court case or another and his revolving around some unusual arrest. Like the woman who stole the five-thousand-dollar ring. The ring had been swiped off the nightstand of a wealthy woman and when Ed and his guys interviewed her in her home, she mentioned that the only person who had access to the house was her maid. There had been no signs of forced entry, so the maid quickly became the prime suspect in the case. Ed brought her in to the station for questioning.

Now it so happens that sitting on Ed's desk was a big, half-gallon masonry jar that the boys at the station had made into a home for two very large spiders. One was black and one was brown and nobody knew what kind they were, but they'd been found outside the station in the bushes and the guys thought they were pretty neat so they more or less adopted them, putting them in the jar with some twigs and leaves and punching holes in the top and feeding the spiders flies from time to time. They kind of became the department's unofficial mascots. The black one was slightly larger than the brown one, about as big as your thumb, but both spiders had leg spans of over three inches.

In any event, the maid was brought into Ed's office for questioning by a detective and when she sat down across from Ed at his desk, she couldn't help but notice the jar and the contents therein.

The woman involuntarily shivered and the detective said, "Oh, I see you've noticed our lie detector spiders."

"Your ... what?"

Ed picked up on what the detective was cooking up. "Uh, yeah," he said, "you see, these aren't just ordinary spiders"

"No?" said the nervous woman.

"They're African spiders," said the detective.

"With special abilities," added Ed.

"Yes," said the detective. "It happens that these spiders have an acute sense of smell."

"Amazing sense of smell," agreed Ed, nodding. "They can actually pick up hormones in the perspiration of a person who is not telling the truth. Isn't that something?"

The woman's jaw dropped open.

"You see," explained the detective, "when a person lies, their body emits a special kind of hormone through the pores of the skin that for whatever reason drives these spiders crazy."

"They attack," added Ed. "They'll bite the person. It's really something else."

The woman's eyes were beginning to bug out.

"Funny thing is," said the detective, "they won't bite if they don't sense that hormone. So if a person's telling the truth, the spiders leave them alone."

"It's really a miracle of nature," Ed said admiringly as he reached for the jar and slid it across the desk towards the woman, slowly turning the lid of the jar. "Now, let's see. You say you don't know anything about the theft of Mrs. Johnson's ring, is that correct?"

"I don't know nothin' about it," the woman said in a quivering voice, averting her eyes from the jar and its occupants.

"Okay, great. Then we should be able to quickly eliminate you as a suspect." By then Ed had taken the lid off the jar and had reached across the desk to take the woman's trembling hand. "If you'd be kind enough to just place your hand into the jar—."

"Okay, okay!" the woman screamed out. "I took the ring! It's in my apartment! In the flour jar on the kitchen counter! Please take them spiders away! *Please!*"

Ed and the detective did everything in their power to keep straight faces and sure enough, upon arriving at the maid's apartment fifteen minutes later and dumping out the contents of the flour jar on her kitchen counter, the ring appeared, dusted with flour but otherwise unharmed.

"I'm afraid we're going to have to place you under arrest, ma'am," said the detective, at which Ed took the detective by the elbow and led him out of earshot of the woman who had begun to sob, the entire ordeal becoming much more than she had bargained for.

"Wait a minute, Jim," said Ed. "Let's think about this for

a second. Imagine this woman pleading guilty in front of the judge and the judge asking her why she's decided to plead. *Because I didn't want to get bit by the lie-detector spiders*?! I don't think so." The detective took Ed's point and the two satisfied themselves with a stern warning to the woman never to steal again and I can't imagine after her introduction to the lie-detector spiders that she ever did.

When they returned the ring to the rightful owner she was thrilled and asked how it was they managed to find it. "Lady," said Ed, "you don't want to know."

⤚

One time, Ed was a big help to me when I got stuck in a tight spot between my role as an attorney for a particular client, and my presumed position as a potential witness in a case that involved that same client. The real issue, however, was an ongoing dispute I had with a rival attorney who I'd beaten in court a time or two before. This was a guy who held a grudge.

He claimed I had information as a witness that would have a bearing on a case that happened to involve my client. It was an ancillary issue to the case at hand and it could be argued—at least he thought so—that my testimony on this issue would not involve a conflict of interest. But I saw it as a definite conflict of interest and, worse, I saw his plan for what it really was—just a feeble attempt to try to frustrate and annoy me. I decided I'd have none of it. I refused to testify as he'd requested. So he tried to have me subpoenaed.

One early winter morning I glanced out of my front window to see a man sitting in his car in my driveway, directly in front of my garage. I had a strong suspicion it had to be a process server and there was no way for me to leave the house without driving past him, upon which I knew I'd be served with the subpoena to appear. As I pondered my course of action, the phone rang. It was Ed.

"Noel," he said, "How about we grab some lunch today?"

"Love to, Ed. But right now I've got a bit of a predicament on my hands." I explained to Ed my situation—my reluctance to testify as a witness in a case involving my client and the grudge-holding attorney who was intent on making me do so.

"Well, then forget lunch," Ed said. "We'll make it breakfast. I'm on my way. Make sure your back door is unlocked."

I did as Ed said and a little while later he came in the rear door, having parked on the block behind mine, jumped my back fence, and trudged his way through a foot of snow in my back yard.

"Just leave it to me," Ed said. "Give me your car keys. And do you still carry that monogrammed briefcase?"

I nodded.

"Let me have that, too," Ed said. Then he headed for the garage and I peered through the window as he pulled my car out, backed it around, and drove past the server's car. The server, by then, had gotten out of his car and was standing in Ed's path. Ed stopped and rolled down the window.

"Good morning," Ed smiled. "What can I do for you?"

"You Noel Gage?"

Ed said nothing, but the server noticed my briefcase on the passenger seat. "N.G." read the monogram.

"Consider yourself served," he said, handing the subpoena to Ed who took it, rolled the window up, and continued on. The server left the premises. Ed came back after driving around the block and the two of us went out and had the breakfast he promised.

Two days later, I was in court with my client. The opposing counsel attempted to call me to the stand.

"Your Honor," I said, "I've not been given any notice to appear today as anybody's witness. I'm here, as the court is no doubt aware, strictly to represent my client."

"Aha!" said the other attorney. "I was afraid you'd pull something like this. Your Honor, contrary to what Mr. Gage claims, he was, indeed, given notice as he was handed a subpoena just the day before yesterday."

"Is this true, Mr. Gage?" asked the judge.

"I'm afraid that my esteemed colleague is incorrect, Your Honor."

"Well it so happens," said the attorney, "that my process server is just outside the courtroom and if it pleases the court, I would very much like to bring him in here and question him under oath about the subpoena in question."

A minute later, the server was on the stand.

"Would you kindly," began the attorney, "point out for the court the individual to whom you served a subpoena two days ago?"

The process server looked all around the courtroom but to no avail.

"I'm sorry. I don't see him here."

The attorney's mouth hung open while I tried my best to stifle a smile. I focused instead on looking bewildered, as if I hadn't a clue what had happened or whom the server had served. The server, meanwhile, stepped down, the trial proceeded, and I never did have to testify. Oh, and I won the case, as well, much to the opposing attorney's chagrin. The next time I got together with Ed, breakfast was on me.

〜

Ed was a family man and one day on some business I

dropped by his house, pulling into his driveway in my new Cadillac de Ville convertible. It was 1968 and Cadillac really knew how to make cars back in those days and this thing was gorgeous. Brown, with a white top and polished chrome everywhere, it had power seats, power windows, cruise control, leather seats, and whitewall tires. In short, it was the whole package.

Ed came out and we talked in his driveway and before long, Ed's thirteen-year-old son came walking out of the house, eyes wide as he ambled around the car, taking it all in. "Wow," I saw him mouth.

"Get in," I offered.

"Really?"

"Sure. Get behind the wheel and check her out." Mike sat in the driver's seat with his hands on the wheel, slowly turning his head around to examine the beautiful interior of the car. "Maybe someday, you'll drive a car like this," I said. Mike nodded hopefully.

A week later, I got a call from Ed.

"Well, you've gone and done it," he said.

"Gone and done what?"

"My in-laws came to visit last night."

"Yeah?"

"And we're sitting around the dinner table and my mother-in-law happens to ask Mike what he wants to do when he gets out of high school. 'I'm going to the University of Michigan,' he says, 'and then Michigan Law School. I'm gonna be a lawyer just like Mr. Gage.' So my mother-in-law asks him what made him decide to do that. Why a lawyer? 'Grandma,' he says to her, 'You should see the car Mr. Gage drives!'"

Well, I suppose there are less noble reasons to get into law. But the fact is that Mike made that decision and never looked back. He's been a lawyer for over thirty years and a damn good one. I'm proud to say he worked part time for me at one point, learning the trade. Smart kid. But I do wonder sometimes what he might be doing today if I hadn't shown up that day in my brand new Cadillac Deville convertible.

⌐

As for Ed, upon his retirement from the force, I suggested he put his detective skills to use. Ed wasn't exactly sure what to do with his time, but he wasn't the kind of guy who'd be satisfied with just sitting around. He needed to do something and he needed to do something productive. So he took my suggestion and became a private investigator and I became his first client, and a regular one at that. As an attorney, you always need solid investigative work done and Ed was effective, efficient, and someone I could trust implicitly.

Sometimes the investigative work you need to have done takes creativity. Ed was good in that way, too. While defending the car manufacturer on a particular case, I was sent to El Paso where the plaintiff of the case resided. I was scheduled to take depositions but I knew I needed some critical information first. One of the depositions was going to be from the plaintiff's chiropractor who claimed his patient's injuries were especially severe. I needed to know what the chiropractor knew. By then, I'd graduated medical school and I knew what to look for: I needed to see the chiropractor's x-rays. And I needed to see the x-rays before the deposition so that I could properly question him about them.

The problem was that the chiropractor was playing hard to get. For several days he eluded me, not taking my calls. Two days before the deposition, I stopped by his office. "I'm sorry, Mr. Gage," said the receptionist. "The doctor is out today. But he has your messages. I'm sure he'll contact you as soon as he's available." I knew better. I suspected the chiropractor was indeed in his office and I began to wonder what it was he was hiding. Why wouldn't he see me or take my calls? Enter Ed Ritenour, P.I.

"Let me go into his office," Ed said when he got off the plane in El Paso the next day. "I'll flush him out." That morning I waited outside the chiropractor's office as Ed walked in, hunched over, moaning in apparent pain.

"May I help you?" the receptionist said.

"I sure hope so," said Ed. "I'm from out of town, working construction on that new building on Mills? Geez, I wrenched my back something awful. I gotta get back on the construction site. I need to see the doc. I can't work like this, that's for sure."

Now I don't know if the chiropractor was especially wary of new patients because of my repeated phone calls, but the receptionist told Ed he was out, just like she'd told me. Ed will tell you that he saw a shadow moving behind the closed door of the doctor's office behind the reception desk. Either way, the receptionist penciled Ed in for an appointment later that afternoon. Maybe the chiropractor figured only a real patient would keep the appointment, who knows? At any rate, Ed hobbled out and we went out for some lunch and killed some time until the appointment time came around.

Once again, I waited in the car out in the parking lot, slinking down in my seat in case the chiropractor happened to glance out. Through the plate glass window of the chiropractor's office, I saw Ed, still hunched over, approach the reception desk and then take a seat in the waiting area. In a few minutes, the receptionist waived him into the doctor's examination room. Ed shot me a quick look out the window. The doctor was in.

That was my cue. I pushed through the front door of the main office and strode right into the doctor's examination room as Ed slid out behind me, not wanting to blow his cover and make the chiropractor realize I'd gained access through questionable means.

"Hi, Doc!" I said, extending my hand. "Noel Gage. Defense attorney? Pleasure to meet you. My, you sure are a tough guy to get in touch with!"

"Well, I —."

"Look, I don't want to keep you. I see you're busy with patients," I said, gesturing toward Ed who was retreating into the waiting area. "Just let me see the x-rays of your patient who was involved in that accident and I'll be on my way and out of your hair!"

The chiropractor was so taken aback that he walked over to his files, rifled through them until he found the file of the plaintiff, and wordlessly handed me the x-rays. I jammed them into the shadowbox and found exactly what I was look- ing for: nothing. Out in the lobby, Ed, still hunched over, watched as I pointed towards the x-rays, delivering what appeared to Ed to be a medical lecture to the chiropractor who was just standing there, taking it in. Then Ed slunk out, saying something to the receptionist about suddenly feeling better. I met up with him in the parking lot.

At the deposition the next day, having been disarmed of whatever theories he might have had about the extent of the plaintiff's injuries, the chiropractor had nothing of sub- stance to testify to. Under oath, he had no choice but to admit that there was essentially no evidence to back up the plaintiff's claims. And when the plaintiff's attorney realized he no longer had a doctor available to present expert testimony in support of his cause of action, he recommended to his client that he drop the case and stop wasting everyone's time.

I'll take only partial credit for the victory. The rest belongs to Ed, a friend I've known now for forty-five years. Great cop, great investigator, a not half-bad actor, and a hell of a guy. Not to mention keeper of the amazing African Lie-Detector Spiders.

CHAPTER NINE

Just a Couple Little Pizza Joints

THE PROCESS SERVER whom Ed successfully thwarted represents a pretty determined, often crafty, group of people. Process servers stop at nothing to accomplish their task: serving subpoenas to people who typically do not want to be served. It's a necessary procedure, of course. Anyone about to become embroiled in a lawsuit has the right to know what's going on. You can't sue somebody, in other words, or call them as a witness, unless they're notified beforehand. But of course it's a lot more convenient for most people to avoid the notification. If you're not notified, how can you be expected to even show up in court? Hence the role of the process server.

We had such a determined server come to our office one time prepared to do whatever it took to serve one of our clients whom he believed to be there. Our front desk and lobby area could be accessed only through a glass door with an electric buzzer. The server stood outside the door motioning to the receptionist that he wanted to come in. The receptionist asked, through an intercom speaker, what his business was. He didn't want to say. So she asked if he had an appointment. Of course he didn't, and she refused him entrance.

No matter. Par for the course for a process server. All in a day's work. He left, walked around to the back of the office, and waited for one of the employees to come out the rear door for the inevitable cigarette break. It didn't take long. A secretary opened the door and the server slipped in behind her before she even realized he'd been waiting there. She turned to question him, but by then he was running into the office area and down a corridor that had offices along the window side and secretaries along the other.

"Hey! Stop!" someone yelled, but the server, ignoring the command, kept going, scanning the name plates on the doors of the offices as he quickly darted past them, looking for the office of the attorney he assumed the client would be in. That's when Mrs. Bloom, a sixty-three-year-old secretary, all of five-feet two-inches and less than a hundred pounds, came scurrying into the corridor ahead of the server, placing herself between him and his determined path.

"You are not allowed back here, young man!" she said. It was a valiant effort by Mrs. Bloom, worthy of employee-of-the-month consideration, but the server ducked to the right and then lunged to the left, gliding right past poor Mrs. Bloom, who stood staring dazedly at the space the server had been occupying just a moment before.

All this time, I happened to be in the conference room talking with some representatives from the Berkley, Michigan police department whom I was representing in labor nego-tiations. We heard the commotion, and one of the representatives, a full-time police officer, ran out into the corridor just as the server was coming past the conference room. Bad timing for the process server. The police officer slammed him up against the wall and then took out his hand-cuffs and slapped them around the server's wrists.

"I'd call this breaking and entering," said the officer. I wanted to agree but the only problem was that my office was in Southfield, out of the officer's jurisdiction. No problem. We called the Southfield P.D., and a Southfield officer came out, swapped handcuffs with the Berkley officer, and took the server down to the station. Unfortunately, that's about as much as we could do. There really wasn't enough to hold him. He was doing his job, after all, even if his methods were a little overly aggressive. For the process server, it was just another day at the office.

⬠

Now, as it happens, watching the whole process server saga unfold in my office that day, while waiting in the lobby for me to finish with the Berkley guys, was a young client by the name of Mike Ilitch. Mike was a small business owner with a couple little pizza joints. The pizza was quite good, as I recall. Mike rented some space in a bar for one of his pizzerias at sixty bucks a month, and the other was in a shopping center where he rented the space at a hundred bucks a month.

I had become Mike's lawyer in a rather odd way. His best friend had been embroiled in a real estate dispute. A transaction had gone badly and Mike's friend was being sued and the plaintiff was none other than a client of mine. The friend was claiming ignorance of real estate law; the case hinged on a technicality that only a bona fide real estate professional could be expected to understand. I deposed Mike's friend, and Mike attended the deposition as moral support for his buddy.

"Sir," I asked, after some quick preliminary questions, "are you a licensed Realtor?" He paused, flushed. How had I known? At length, he managed a timid "yes." That was enough for me. It was, perhaps, the shortest deposition of my career. Mike's friend could no longer plead ignorance. He had had the advantage in the transaction, an advantage born of knowledge he claimed he didn't have. His side quickly settled.

To this day, I don't know what made me think to ask the man if he was a Realtor. Instinct, I suppose. A hunch. Back in the pre-Internet days there was no way to just Google someone to learn all about them. There was nothing to indicate the man was licensed, and his claim of ignorance with respect to the details of the transaction seemed to preclude the idea. But I asked anyway and the result was a success. Sometimes things work out like that.

Mike was a smart guy. I had prevailed over his best friend, but Mike knew that business was business and he wasn't about to hold the result of the action against me. In Mike's eyes, I had just done my job and I had done it well. So well that he called me the next day to tell me that I was his new attorney. I said thanks and told him I looked forward to working with him and didn't think much more about it. The guy only owned two small pizza joints, after all. Not a person that I anticipated as being in frequent need of a lawyer.

That was in the 1960s. As it turns out, the pizza places were called Little Caesar's. Today, Mike Ilitch and his Little Caesar's empire are worth billions of dollars. His holdings, besides the pizza operation, include the Detroit Red Wings and the Detroit Tigers.

Mike got so big, in fact, that he eventually outgrew my law firm. He needed more than what we could reasonably offer. But while he was my client, we had some interesting cases, one of which involved the Red Wings. One of their star players, a defenseman with a huge free-agent contract, went down to injury shortly after the Wings acquired him. The contract was guaranteed, and the player claimed he could no longer play. The Wings were on the hook for over twelve million dollars.

Mike got a hold of me and said he felt the injury was not nearly as serious as the player was claiming. In fact, the player was known to own sled dogs and was an active participant in dogsled racing, an activity as grueling as ice hockey. In Mike's mind, the player should have been out on the ice helping his team.

"What can we do?" Mike asked. I told him I'd come up with something. Then I hired a private plane to fly over the player's ten-acre property and take photographs. Sure enough, there was the player, out in the snow training his dogs. This bolstered Mike's case immensely. The news hit the papers and the response was more or less split. A lot of fans were upset at the player and a lot of fans were upset at me for "invasion of privacy." But of course you have no reasonable expectation of privacy if you're outside in the woods. You're fair game.

In any event, the player and the team agreed to arbitration and they ultimately settled. I was happy I could help, regardless of the shots I took from the media. Mike was a great guy and so is his wife Marian. Hilda and I became good friends with them and we travelled together as families. They eventually had seven kids and I remember Denise in particular, who was just a little girl when I knew her. She has now gone on to have a very successful law career. Each of the children owns shares in the Red Wings and because of that, their names are engraved on a very special piece of hardware. Mike's Wings were NHL champions in 1997, 1998, 2002, and 2008. And so you can find the Ilitch name repeatedly on the legendary Stanley Cup; well deserved, if you ask me. All in all, I'd have to say Mike's had a pretty good career for a guy who started out with just a couple pizza joints.

CHAPTER TEN

My Time as a Business Mogul

MIKE ILITCH OWNED the Detroit Tigers, along with the Red Wings, but long before he came along, the team was owned by Walter Briggs, Senior. In fact, from 1938 to 1961, old Tiger Stadium was actually called Briggs Stadium and in that time the Tigers won two American League Pennants and a World Series. I knew Walter's grandson, Mickey Briggs. Though Mickey was a Harvard-educated attorney, he never really practiced law. He owned some businesses and brought a lot of his legal work to me. Mickey and I became good friends.

One of the businesses Mickey owned was a one-hundred-employee company called Huron Die Casting. The name was a bit misleading as its major source of revenue was from plastic manufacturing, about half of which comprised plastic parts sold to the automotive industry. To settle some legal issues, Mickey found himself needing to divest his portfolio of Huron, and quickly. And so he came to me.

"Noel," he said, "I need to sell one of my companies. Huron Die Casting."

"Well, Mickey," I replied, "I'd love to help. But you know, that's not really my thing. I'm a trial attorney. Maybe I can refer you to someone who would be more knowledgeable about the sale of a business."

"No, no," he said, shaking his head. "I don't need a lawyer, Noel. I need a buyer."

"A buyer? You mean ... me?"

"Sure, why not?"

"But, Mickey, I don't have the money to buy your company. Nor would I know anything about running it."

"Don't worry about a thing," Mickey said. "I've got it all set up. I've arranged a bank loan for you. The company's doing well and the income will more than offset the debt service on the loan. And if doesn't, I'm going to back up the loan so you'll have exactly zero financial exposure."

"But what about running it? The day-to-day details? Mickey, I'm running a law practice."

"What running it? There's no running it. Noel, that's what the managers do. I got some fine people in place. You won't have to do a thing." Then he paused and said, "Noel, I really need you to help me out here. Will you take the company off my hands?"

"Mickey," I said, "if you really need me to, I will. But only if you're sure the managers will stay on."

"Positive." We shook hands and filed all the paperwork and the next thing you know, I was the owner of a manufacturing company.

It took exactly one week for all the managers to leave.

They scurried like rats off a sinking ship, operating under the general perception that Mickey's selling the company meant it was going down. It wasn't, at least so far as I could tell; Mickey had sold for legal, not business, reasons. In any event, I was now forced to take a more hands-on approach to a business I knew nothing about. With nowhere else to turn, I called upon my brother.

Leslie William Gage, five and a half years older than I am, had earned two college degrees by the age of seventeen: one, an electrical engineering degree from Cooper Union and the other an English degree from Queens College. At

Queens, he finished first in his class but he was maddened by the fact that at Cooper Union, he had only finished second. My brother didn't care much for second place. After college, he began his career as a technical writer but would eventually go on to work for the Atomic Energy Commission, which would ultimately become the Nuclear Regulatory Commission.

We were never close, my brother and I, although I've developed a great relationship with his son, Daniel. My nephew is a terrific young man, currently employed by the State Department. His father—my brother—was a bona fide genius. Once we took a trip to Vegas together, staying at the Sands where I'd stayed with Tom Sullivan years before. Les didn't approve of gambling but agreed to help me win at blackjack. I think he liked the challenge as well as the ability to demonstrate his mental capabilities. I sat at the blackjack table in the casino while he stood behind me, mentally calculating the odds that at any given time, taking into consideration what had already been dealt, a card worth ten points would turn up. When I started winning big, the casino made my brother leave.

At any rate, during some vacation time at the NRC, Leslie agreed to come look things over at Huron Die. I figured if anybody could properly analyze a business, it would be him. What he found wasn't good. Not only were the financial numbers abysmal, but there were problems with the employees. One morning, Leslie spotted a woman sprawled out on top of one of the machines, sound asleep. "Is this really the best place for a nap?" he asked after shaking her awake.

"But I was on a break!" she declared.

That was more or less all Leslie needed to see. "This company can't survive," he told me and then he turned and walked out of the office, heading back for Washington and leaving me to deal with a failing company.

Though I might not have had any experience running a company, I knew how to read financials. I found a few places we could cut some fat and I made some hard decisions. For one thing, we had a guy on the payroll who was acting more in the capacity of a factory rep than an employee. As such, he was taking a salary when he should have been on commission. I restructured the sales department and effectively terminated his position. What I didn't know was that this guy had a pretty powerful friend named Dollie Cole.

In Detroit, everyone knew who Dollie was. She was the wife of Ed Cole, President of General Motors, but she was much more than that. A popular socialite, Dollie was outspoken and well-respected in her own right. "The strongest muscle in my body is my mouth," she once told the *New York Times*. And she meant it. Dollie was the kind of person who got things done. Ed had a motto he lived by and Dollie lived by it, too: "Kick the hell out of the status quo." The two were perfect for each other and made a great team. Both worked hard. Dollie once joked that when they were married, the minister should have said, "I now pronounce you man and wife and briefcase."

At any rate, one day shortly after I fired the factory rep, I received a call from Dollie Cole.

"Mr. Gage," she said, "You fired a friend of mine."

"I did?"

"Yes, and he needs his job back."

I explained the situation. It was a necessary cost-cutting measure.

"Well, look, Mr. Gage," she said, "I happen to know you don't have any expertise or experience in running a company."

"Well, maybe not, but—."

94

"Mr. Gage, why don't I run the company for you?"

"I'm sorry?"

"You heard me, Mr. Gage. Let me run the company. I have contacts all over the world. I'm sure we can be extremely successful."

How could I refuse? I didn't want the company to begin with. And Dollie wasn't kidding about her contacts. Her husband, I would come to learn, had the personal, direct phone number of President Nixon. As Chairman of Huron, I made the best business decision I could have made: I made Dollie Cole the president.

For a short time, we turned things around. But by the late 1970s, times were hard. The oil crisis was hurting the automotive industry and we weren't getting nearly the same amount of business. On top of that, oil, as it happens, is a necessary ingredient for polypropylene which, in turn, was a necessary ingredient for the plastic parts we manufactured. Polypropylene was in short supply and we were hurting.

"Dollie," I said one day over lunch, "what are we going to do? Where are we going to get our polypropylene?"

Dollie thought for a moment. "I can get us what we need," she said.

"You can? Where?"

"Rochester."

"Rochester?"

"We'll fly there in the morning. Meet me at the airport at 9:00."

What I didn't know was that Dollie was good friends with Walter Fallon, CEO of Eastman Kodak. Kodak had been doing business with GM and Kodak had polypropylene. Fallon felt obliged to help Dollie get the polypropylene we needed and we managed to keep the business going.

Unfortunately, even though we now had better access

to our raw material, even Dollie couldn't do anything about the overall economy. The U.S. automobile industry was in a serious state of decline and with it, so was our business. We made repeated staff cuts until only a skeletal crew remained and, eventually, there wasn't even enough work for the skeletal crew. I ended up turning the building into warehouse space and ultimately selling it off. So ended Huron Manufacturing.

⤷

But with the loss of the company, I had at least picked up a friend in Dollie and, in time, a client in her husband Ed. Being Ed Cole's attorney was challenging and fun and, in one particular case, potentially very lucrative.

"Pick me up tomorrow morning," he said one day on the phone to me. "We're flying to Chicago. I'm going to buy Avis Rent-a-Car."

At the time, Avis was owned by International Telephone & Telegraph Corporation. ITT was big and getting bigger. In 1963, they'd attempted to buy ABC but the deal was halted by federal antitrust regulators. So ITT decided to grow by buying companies outside of the telecommunications industry, a strategy presumably acceptable to the government. They bought Sheraton Hotels, Wonder Bread, Avis, and about 300 other companies all throughout the 1960s. But when they attempted to buy Hartford Insurance in 1970, the U.S. Justice Department stepped in. Hartford was just a little too big for comfort. The Justice Department allowed the acquisition, but forced ITT to divest itself of assets the value of which would be equivalent to the acquisition price of Hartford. One of those assets was Avis.

Ed's idea was to replace all the Avis cars with General

Motors cars. By then, he'd retired as CEO but after more than forty-four years of employment, his loyalty remained strong. But as smart as Ed was, he couldn't pull off the deal for Avis by himself. And so he enlisted a couple partners. One was a hugely successful Cadillac dealer out of New York named Victor Potamkin. Potamkin had started as a Chevy dealer with franchises in Philadelphia, Miami, and Newark. In 1972, Ed Cole and GM talked him into taking over the fledgling, company-owned Cadillac store in Manhattan. The move was a huge success and Potamkin expanded. Eventually, he'd become the largest Cadillac dealer in the world, with an empire that included fifty-four dealerships in several states and $1.2 billion in sales.

But the other partner was the real money man: A.N. Pritzker from Chicago. The Prizker name was well-known. The Pritzker family had amassed a fortune, mostly through real estate. Back in 1957, Pritzker's sons, continuing to build on their father's business, bought a hotel in Los Angeles called the Hyatt House. The rest, as they say, is history. The Hyatt hotel chain grew into one of the largest hotel chains in the world. But the Pritzker group owned other businesses as well and A.N. was willing to add Avis into the mix.

So the morning after Ed's call, I drove over to his house to pick him up as instructed. We were going to Chicago with Potamkin to meet with Pritzker and put the deal together. Now, the thing is, I owned a Lincoln Continental at the time. I also owned a General Motors Pontiac but, thinking the Continental would be a more comfortable ride, and completely forgetting exactly who it was I was picking up, I left the Pontiac in the garage. Ed walked out of his house when I pulled up and took a look at the Continental.

"Noel," he said, "I thought you were going to drive us to the airport."

"I am," I replied.

"In that piece of crap?"

I was humiliated. There I was on the doorstep of the former CEO of General Motors with a Ford car! Ed Cole was going to be driven to the airport in a car of GM's biggest competitor.

"Oh, Ed," I said, "I'm sorry. I really wasn't thinking."

"Forget it," he said. "Let's get going." And that was all that was said; but I couldn't imagine Ed was too thrilled with my car of choice. I considered apologizing again but then decided that letting the matter drop might be the best and quickest way to put it in the past. And so we drove to the airport—Pontiac Municipal, ironically—where the private jet was waiting for us. Potamkin was already aboard, the flight having originated in New York.

The three of us flew to Chicago and met Pritzker in (where else?) the downtown Hyatt. By then, Ed had taken me aside to let me know his plans for compensating me.

"For putting this thing together, Noel, and walking it through all the legal hurdles, I'm cutting you in for five percent. Does that sound okay?"

Did it sound okay? Avis was a multimillion dollar company. Five percent sounded better than okay. Five percent would be life changing.

The problem, however, was the money man. A.N. Pritzker was a tough, shrewd businessman. And conservative. He wouldn't agree to buy Avis for anything close to what ITT wanted. And Cole and Potamkin could not convince him otherwise. We made our offer, ITT turned it down, and then ITT found another buyer. The real tragedy was that just a few years later, the buyer resold Avis for a multiple of what we could have had it for. To this day, I think about the lost opportunity.

I did get one thing out of the experience, however. The day after we returned from Chicago to Detroit, I woke up to find a brand new Cadillac in my driveway with a note from Ed Cole tucked under the driver's side windshield wiper: "Yours if you get rid of that piece of crap. —E.C." I dumped the Lincoln that afternoon.

Ed couldn't sit idly in retirement. The only reason he'd left GM was due to a mandatory retirement rule. He'd turned sixty-five and had to turn the reins of the company over to a younger man. But Ed kept going. When the Avis deal didn't work out, he bought into and became CEO of Checker Motor Corporation in Kalamazoo, manufacturer of the ubiquitous Checker cab. One evening in May of 1977, he and Dollie were over at my house for dinner. Ed was telling me about his plans.

"We're going to update the Checker," he explained. "Basically, we're going to use the bodies of Volkswagens. But we're going to cut them in half, insert a section to make them longer, and raise the roofs. We're modernizing the look. Listen, I'm flying my plane to Kalamazoo tomorrow. Why don't you come with me?" Ed had a twin-engine British Beagle and he'd been flying for years. He knew I was a student pilot. "You can be my copilot, and I'd love to show you the Checker operation."

"Sounds great, Ed, but I have to be in court tomorrow for a hearing. Besides, the weather's supposed to be terrible tomorrow. You shouldn't be flying. They're predicting severe thunderstorms."

"Bah. I've flown through worse."

"Well, I'm sure you have, but it's only a couple hours by

car. Why take the chance?"

Ed waved a hand and we talked more about his plans for Checker and various other subjects before he and Dollie said their goodnights.

I got a call from a tearful Dollie the next day. Ed's plane had gone down. He had flown right into the path of a storm. Ed Cole was sixty-seven.

For the next five years my final act as Ed's attorney was to defend his estate from all manner of people who came out of the woodwork. People that Dollie assumed were friends of Ed's were suddenly making claims. His tennis partner swore that he and Ed had made a handshake deal on a real estate project. The partner had made financial commitments based on Ed's supposed word. There were a lot of these unprovable claims and it was hard seeing Dollie have to deal with them at the same time she was trying to come to terms with her husband's death. I was glad I could help. The statute of frauds requires real estate contracts, among other types of agreements, to be in writing; the handshake deals were pretty easy to dispense with. Nevertheless, it was time-consuming and more than a little disheartening for Dollie.

⌒

Now it turns out that even though Ed's General Motors may have been locked in mortal business combat with Ford Motors (producing the necessity of me having to rid myself of my Lincoln), that didn't keep the wives from socializing together. Dollie was good friends with Cristina Ford, second wife of Henry Ford II, CEO of Ford and grandson of the founder. HF2, as he was sometimes known, was divorcing Cristina, and Dollie thought I might be able to help Cristina with some legal advice. Divorce wasn't exactly my thing, but

Cristina was well represented by another attorney and was only looking for a second opinion about some of the particulars. She needed some basic questions answered and I agreed to help. Dollie and I were invited to Ford's mansion in Grosse Pointe for dinner. By then, Henry had moved out.

The house was massive, and was, in fact, one of the sticking points in the divorce negotiations. Cristina apologized for the fact that HF2 had removed most of the staff. "Only" half a dozen house staff members had stayed, including the butler. Though the butler had remained, he also remained steadfastly loyal to Henry, something I found out when Cristina suggested I select a bottle of wine.

"Dollie tells me you know your wine," she said.

"Well, I like to think so," I admitted.

"James, please take Mr. Gage down to the wine cellar and let him pick out whatever bottle he recommends for dinner." But when we got down to the wine cellar, I noticed "James" positioning himself between me and a certain area of the cellar that housed the best of Henry's wine collection.

"Those look interesting," I said, pointing to the shelves behind James. I started to move around him but he moved with me.

"Yes sir, I'm sure they are, but I think you'll find something to your liking right here," he said, waving to the more pedestrian bottles. I took the hint. But dinner was fine and Cristina somehow managed to be a gracious host, soldiering through the serving of dinner and dessert, handicapped as she was by the skeletal crew of six.

Working with people like Cristina Ford and A.N. Pritzker, Victor Potamkin, and Mickey Briggs, and (of course) Ed and Dollie Cole, was a fascinating experience, both professionally and personally. I was almost made part owner of a major car rental corporation and I ran, with help and to the best of my ability such as it was, a plastics manufacturing company. The world of business had made its calling. But the world of law was still my home.

CHAPTER ELEVEN
Hazards of the Profession

JUST BECAUSE I WAS more comfortable in the legal world than the business world doesn't mean I didn't dabble in business ventures from time to time. I was making money and so I naturally had an interest in investing it successfully. My offices at one time, for instance, were housed in a building I owned in partnership with two real estate developers and the deal ended up being a very profitable investment.

One of the partners built a lakefront home for Hilda and me. Hilda had it decorated with custom furniture that she'd ordered for the home. The furniture didn't come cheap, which is what made it all the more tragic when it was all lost in a fire. The fire, as it happened, was not at the lake house. The lake house is still there, so far as I know. Hilda and I owned the home for a while, then eventually sold it, taking the furniture and putting it into public storage in a large warehouse where it was to be kept safe and secure until we would one day decide what to do with it. I paid my monthly storage fee and thought nothing of it.

One day, a few years after we had sold the lake house, I was visited by a potential client, who was in some serious criminal trouble and out on bond. The man was facing an arson charge. He had a sad history of pyromania, and his latest conflagration led the police to his door where he was arrested and facing significant jail time. The investigation had been ongoing and it had taken almost a year for the cops to put the pieces together. Now, it appeared they had their man.

I listened to the firebug's request for representation and then asked, "What was it that you torched exactly?"

"Oh, a public storage warehouse," he said.

"Uh-huh. Whereabouts?"

"One of the places out by the airport."

"Oh? Which one?"

A couple more questions back and forth and a sudden, sickening realization hit me, causing me to ask this: "Just how bad *was* this fire?"

"Oh, it scorched everything," he declared. "Nothing at all left. Burned everything to the ground."

For close to a year, I'd been paying a monthly storage fee for a warehouse that no longer existed to store furniture that also no longer existed.

"Look, I'm afraid I can't represent you," I told the arsonist.

"Why not?"

"I have a bit of a conflict of interest." What happened to him, I don't know. My interest was the company who owned the warehouse. I couldn't exactly blame the pyromaniac for starting a fire. It was deplorable but that's what pyromaniacs do. But it's also why a public storage company ought to have adequate security and sprinklers and alarms and proper firefighting procedures. Even at that, I understand that sometimes things happen beyond one's ability to control them. That's just the way things are. But continuing to take payments from me for months after my property was completely destroyed? This was inconceivable.

In the end, I made the company not only reimburse me for the monthly payments, but for the cost of the furniture, too. Sometimes I marvel at the coincidence and wonder how much longer I would have made those monthly payments had I not opened my office door one day to an arsonist who just happened to have picked, of all warehouses, the warehouse where Hilda's custom furniture was being stored.

Meanwhile, George, the builder who had built the lake house, was having problems of his own. He'd been having an affair with a woman whose husband was coming a bit unhinged by his wife's betrayal. He'd found out about George and had begun to stalk him. The man was jealous and he was dangerous. George came to me for advice.

"Simple!" I said. "Stop seeing her! She's married. And so are you!" What made the whole thing somehow worse was that George's wife was strikingly good-looking. His mistress, on the other hand, wasn't attractive at all. Not that beauty is a legitimate reason for adultery, but at least it makes it a bit more understandable. Either way, George was in deep and he needed to get out.

"Well, I like her," he said by way of defense. Unattractive as she was, I guess her husband liked her, too, what with his agitation over the affair. She must have had something going for her and I could only surmise that she had knowledge of some kind of magical bedroom technique that had previously been unknown to mankind.

George didn't listen to me. Nor did he listen to a mutual friend of ours—Chief of Police Ed Ritenour, who told George basically the same thing I'd told him. Our advice fell on deaf ears, and the result was tragic.

Sitting with the woman in his car one night in a parking lot, George was approached by the woman's husband who had been following them. The husband was armed with a shotgun. He rapped on George's window and lifted the shotgun to the level of George's head. George rolled down the window.

"What do you want?" he said.

"I want you to stop seeing my wife!" the man replied. Then George, with just a slight streak of arrogance as usual, presented the man with what we in the legal profession call the *digitus impudicus*. The middle finger. It was one step too far. The man squeezed the trigger. At the trial for the senseless murder of my friend, his lawyers would plead the husband guilty to manslaughter.

⤳

Though I never had a shotgun pointed at me, let alone fired in my direction, when you're an attorney, especially a trial attorney, you often make enemies, almost by definition. It's the nature of the game. After all, you're taking an adversarial position on each case. Sometimes, when an adversary doesn't understand that you're just doing your job and that it's nothing personal, things can get a little tense. Sometimes hazardous. Sometimes just plain dangerous.

So it was with a large hulk of a man who hailed from New York. It seems the man's wife had been having an affair. Rather than resort to the shotgun, this man's revenge was to try to have his wife prosecuted for adultery. In Michigan, to this very day, adultery is a felony. It's an antiquated law, of course, one of those laws instituted back in the early days of the state's history. There's also a law on the books that a married woman isn't allowed to cut her own hair without her husband's permission and a law in Detroit that says you're not allowed to let your pig run loose on the streets. Nobody ever gets prosecuted for breaking these laws, of course. It's just that nobody's ever bothered to take the time to have them repealed.

In any event, the large man from New York decided he

was going to file a complaint of adultery against his wife. But he first needed evidence. So he set her up, telling her he was traveling back to New York for business. He said goodbye, walked out of their Oakland County, Michigan home, got in his car, and began driving towards the airport. But then he took a detour to his brother's apartment and the two drove back to the house where they hid in the backyard behind some bushes, just waiting for the wife's lover to arrive. An hour later he did, and that's when the fun began.

The husband and his brother stormed into the house with the brother snapping pictures of the wife and lover together in a very compromising, very intimate position. The stunned lover somehow managed to get his clothes on and scramble out the front door but the poor wife was stuck in the bedroom where the husband actually pried her legs apart and made the brother take more pictures. I guess the idea was to show that she had, indeed, been naked with the lover but, when the pictures were presented as evidence, it just looked to me like a brazen, clumsy attempt to humiliate.

I became involved when the wife's father called our firm looking to get his daughter out of a jam. The husband, photographic evidence in hand, had gone to the police insisting on pressing charges. The police, reluctantly, had no choice but to arrest the woman. There was a law on the books, after all, no matter how antiquated it might have been. At the arraignment, which the husband took the time to attend, I entered a plea for the woman of not guilty.

"This is a waste of the court's time," I told the judge. "Certainly our judicial system is set up for more important matters than this. This man," I added, pointing towards the husband, "is feeling betrayed by his wife and rather than face the fact that she is obviously no longer in love with him, he is instead trying to exact retribution in such a misguided, pitiable way that he has confirmed in everybody's mind here today the reasoning behind the loss of this woman's love for him. Certainly this man's behavior cannot be tolerated." I could feel the man fuming.

"Well, I'm inclined to agree," said the judge. "I have no interest in binding this matter over for trial. The court is not the proper venue for a betrayed spouse to air his grievances. This case is dismissed."

That should have been that. But on the way out of the courtroom, the man, still fuming and now with no legal recourse against his wandering wife, decided to take out his aggression on me. In his mind, somebody had to pay and I was a convenient target.

"You son of a bitch!" he bellowed as he lunged at me. I sidestepped him and then he made a big roundhouse of a swing with his right fist that would, should he have made contact, definitely have laid me out cold. I managed to duck the swing just in time and the man, now off-balance, was subdued by the bailiff and two cops. And then he was led off to jail. I never learned exactly what became of him, but I understand he ended up paying a small fortune in alimony when his divorce was ultimately settled.

⌣

That wouldn't be the last time somebody took umbrage at my adversarial efforts. I had a man actually attempt to assault me from the witness stand. My client—a Playboy bunny—was suing the man for paternity. I didn't like him from the beginning. It was clear from the evidence that he was the father of her child; not only was that the case, but also she was a magnificent creature, beautiful and warm and smart. This man had made promises to her, used her, and then dumped her. I could find no redeeming qualities at all in him.

Once it was determined that the man was the father, the matter of how much child support should be paid became the issue before the court and I was determined to make the man pay and pay big. I knew he owned a successful department store and was wealthy. It was my job to reveal the evidence that would show just how wealthy he was. I did this simply by putting the man on the stand and asking him questions about his income, his two houses, his cars, his trips to Europe, and everything else I'd managed to dig up about him. He tried to skirt the questions, answering in the vaguest of terms. "Well, sure I have a beach house," he said at one point, "but it's very tiny. No more than a shack, really."

The judge meanwhile was a no-nonsense woman whom I had been in front of before on several occasions. She didn't allow the man to get away with his answers and I continued to hammer away at him, laying him bare as he reluctantly divulged his financial capabilities.

Before long, reluctance made way for frustration and frustration made way for fury. Little by little, I could see the man was losing control of his emotions. Suddenly, he erupted, coming off the stand and steaming towards me. He didn't get very far. The bailiff grabbed him while the judge banged her gavel down repeatedly. Now the fury made its way to her.

"Do not test this court," she admonished the man, "or you will experience the consequences and I can assure you that you will not like them. I would be more than happy to hold you in contempt of court if that is what you would like, sir, leaving you in a cell where you will have all the time you need to consider your actions and find a way to control your outbursts. Do we understand each other?"

The man was compliant from that point forward, but

naturally the incident didn't help him when it came time for the judge to render her decision for the amount of child support. Let's just say the Playboy bunny was well taken care of.

⌒

Sometimes the anger comes not from the adversary but from the adversary's attorney. You'd expect better from an educated professional, but better isn't always what you get. Attorneys are people, too. And it's not always some young hothead, either. In a probate case one day I happened to come up against a veteran lawyer who must have been pushing seventy. But for all his years of experience, it turned out that he wasn't very knowledgeable about the rules of evidence in probate cases, particularly the cases that went before a jury. This was not a complete surprise, actually, as this specific case happened to be the first probate case in Oakland County to make use of a jury. Up until then, cases were tried only in front of a judge. But the law had just been changed.

My venerable opponent's experience was such that he was able in the past to play fairly fast and loose with the rules of evidence in front of judges who might be inclined to provide a certain amount of latitude. With a jury, however, things are a little tighter. Processes and procedures are not so relaxed. For my part, I was well-versed in the proper rules of evidence and I felt it my duty to object whenever opposing counsel would try to submit evidence that did not comport with those rules. The judge had no choice but to sustain my objections. And there were several of them. The attorney simply hadn't done his homework. The sudden shift to a more formal trial process threw him for a loop and he was unprepared. It showed. The trial turned into something of an embarrassment for him. He became angry but instead of being angry at himself for not knowing the rules, he naturally turned his ire towards me.

"Once again, Your Honor," I said at one point, for probably about the tenth time, "I'm going to have to raise an objection to my colleague's attempt to submit this exhibit as evidence."

The judge sighed. "And once again, I'm going to have to sustain your objection, counselor. I cannot allow this as evidence."

"Okay, that's *it!*" the opposing attorney blurted out. "I've had it! I can see what's going on here. This is becoming a sham. I'm not going to get any justice for my client here, it's obvious! Well, you know what? I'll get some justice. I'll just take it into my own hands!"

With that, the attorney strode over to me and took a swing not unlike the roundhouse from the jilted New Yorker. I stepped aside but managed to grab his arm and spin him completely around until we were staring each other face to face.

"Now look," I said. "I don't want to hurt you. But I'm a hell of a lot younger than you and quicker, too. You take another swing at me and I *will* flatten you right here and now."

There was no bailiff in the probate court and by then the judge had run out of the courtroom in search of an officer. He ran down the hall of the courthouse and managed to grab a county sheriff who stormed in and took the offending attorney away. Order was restored, and by what specific authority I don't exactly remember, but the case was ruled in my favor, the outburst having marked the end of the case. I went home happy to have won the case and happier still that I had managed to avoid a fist that had been aimed squarely at my face. All in a day's work, I suppose.

CHAPTER TWELVE

More Hazards of the Profession

IT WASN'T ALWAYS JUST fists that got thrown my way. One day, on the twentieth floor of the Cadillac Tower in downtown Detroit, I found myself deposing another attorney's client. The attorney didn't much care for my line of questioning; the answers weren't exactly favorable to his client. He kept objecting but the questions were pertinent and reasonable and I just kept letting him object while I continued the questioning. I could see he was getting more and more irritated.

"You don't have to answer that," he would say to his client.

"I'm afraid you do," I'd correct, "and please remember that you're under oath."

Maybe the attorney was just frustrated, I don't know. Or maybe there was something else going on in his life that was bothering him. Maybe he was having problems at home. Maybe his kids were getting into trouble or something. Or maybe he was just having a bad day. Who can say? All I know for sure is that somewhere about thirty minutes into the deposition, the attorney grabbed a telephone that was sitting on his end of the conference table, yanked it so hard that the cord came out of the wall, and hurled it towards me as I sat at the opposite end of the table. This was in the early 1970s, before cell phones and even before light plastic phones. Heck, this was back in the rotary phone days. The phone was a big, black, heavy thing. Get hit in the head with one of those and you'd be knocked silly. I ducked right in time.

The problem, however, was that my end of the conference table placed me with my back to the window. And it was summer. The Cadillac Tower didn't have air conditioning at the time or, if it did, it wasn't in use on that particular day. The windows were open instead, which is something you could still do with windows in office towers back in those times. These particular windows opened from the bottom and I recollect this one being opened about the height of, well, about the height of an old-style rotary phone, as a matter of fact. An inch either way and the phone would have hit the window or the wall and probably just dropped to the floor of the conference room. The attorney could not have made a better throw if he had tried; the phone sailed perfectly through the open window, the ripped cord trailing it downward like the tail of a kite.

Twenty floors down the phone went. I held my breath and turned and glanced tentatively out of the window towards the street, imagining the worst—some poor soul walking along, struck in the head by a falling object that he would never have seen coming. For an instant I even imagined the bell ringing (appropriately, I suppose) upon impact. The unfortunate pedestrian would be sprawled out face first on the pavement, posing for the inevitable chalk outline the investigating police officer would draw around him.

Fortunately the phone was lying harmlessly in pieces upon the sidewalk, having missed any chance passerby.

The room went silent. "I have no further questions at this time," I finally said.

It wasn't always in the line of work that I found myself in dangerous spots. Twice I was assaulted outside the courtroom and both times I was able to defend myself with a concealed weapon that I had a permit to carry. Once was by a would-be mugger outside a clothiers on Washington Boulevard in downtown Detroit. He sidled up to me seemingly out of nowhere. *Your money or your life*, the guy said, just like in the movies. In his hand was a large, shiny knife. I pulled my trench coat back to reveal my Smith & Wesson sitting in a holster on my hip.

"Take your chances," I said. The mugger paused just a moment and then turned and ran. My move had more or less been instinctual but in retrospect, it might not have been the smartest move to make. I thought later that evening that the mugger could easily have lunged at me and driven that knife home before I'd have any chance at all of pulling the gun out of its holster. Needless to say, after that thought occurred to me, I didn't sleep very well that night.

The Smith & Wesson, as it happens, was a pearl-handled gift I'd been presented with the very night before by the Beverly Hills (Michigan) Police Officers Association. I had recently represented them in a labor dispute. There was a statute in those days that police officers couldn't go on strike, leaving them little recourse where compensation was concerned. They had to take what they got, and that was pretty much that. I tried to negotiate on their behalf, but without the threat of striking, you don't really have the best hand to play. Finally, I told the city managers this: "These officers are brave and dutiful public servants and they deserve to be paid accordingly. And not only do they deserve it, but their very careers require it. They need, for example, access to decent healthcare. But that costs money. Not getting paid appropriately, they can't afford properly skilled doctors. And, look, here it is the cold and flu season. Unfortunate timing, wouldn't you say? I mean, imagine what would happen if all the officers got sick and they couldn't afford medical treatment and they all had to stay home. Without a pay raise, that's a distinct possibility. They all could come down with the flu and have to call in sick. All of them. At the same time. On the same day."

I didn't need to spell it out any further. The city got the message. You weren't allowed to strike but there was no law that prohibited you from calling in sick. The threat of the "blue flu" was enough to induce a nice-sized (well-deserved) raise in pay for the Beverly Hills officers and they were very grateful. Hence, the pearl-handled Smith & Wesson. In fact, it was my success there that led to my representation of the Southfield Police Officers Association where, of course, I met Ed Ritenour.

꙳

I also carried a .22 caliber Bernadelli back in those days and that came in handy one day, too. I was driving in Southfield late one afternoon in pretty heavy traffic, navigating an access road that ran beside the freeway. Out of the corner of my eye, towards my left, I suddenly saw a car exiting the freeway and merging onto the access road apparently oblivious to my presence. Fearing I was about to be sideswiped, I hit the horn. The driver saw me just in time and made enough of a correction to avoid hitting me. As I glanced over, I could see the reason for his distraction. He had his left hand on the wheel of the car and his right hand underneath the blouse of his girlfriend who was sitting next to him.

The horn apparently angered him. He swerved in front of me and two blocks later we came up to a red light. That's when he got out of his car and walked back towards me, rapping on my driver's side window.

"Get out of the car!" he said. I looked straight ahead, windows rolled up, doors locked. I didn't want any trouble. I knew the guy was probably just trying to impress his girlfriend.

I waited for the light to turn green, assuming the man would go back to his car and that would be the end of it. He'd go his way, I'd go mine. But when the light turned green, the guy didn't move. "Get out of the car," he said again, "or I'm going to come through the window."

I turned towards him. "Suit yourself," I said and then I opened up the glove box, retrieved the .22 Bernadelli I'd had resting inside it, and sat the Bernadelli on my lap. The guy looked at the gun. Then he looked back at his girlfriend who'd been watching the whole thing. Then he looked at me with a sort of questioning expression, and then he looked at the gun again. Then he walked back to his car and took off. I don't imagine his girlfriend was very impressed.

As it happens, I'd been on my way to the Beverly Hills Police Department on business (another wage negotiation). When I got there fifteen minutes after the incident, I casually mentioned the whole thing to Sergeant Lutz, a good guy who took exception to the idea of somebody treating "his" lawyer that way.

"He did what?!" said Sergeant Lutz. "He can't do that to our guy. Nobody does that to our guy. Did you happen to get his license number?" As a matter of fact I had and I gave it to Sergeant Lutz and I thought no more about it.

But the very next day I got a phone call from Milton Sackett, Southfield Chief of Police. "Say, Noel," Milton said, "I got a guy here wants to file a felony report on you. Said that out of nowhere you pulled a weapon and pointed it at him yesterday. Know anything about what he's talking about?"

I laughed and filled Milton in on just exactly what had transpired on the access road the day before—the fact that I'd almost been hit, the threatening words and actions of the driver, even about the girlfriend and the open blouse.

"I see," said Milton. "No problem, Noel. We'll take care of it."

"Sure, Milt. By the way, you might remind the man that it's a felony in the state of Michigan to file a false felony report."

"Yep," said Milton. "I was gonna do just that." And after Milton explained the ramifications, the guy apparently split, mumbling something about how he'd think the matter over and "get back" to Milton in due time.

Now, later that day in the course of my business I needed to make a phone call to the Beverly Hills P.D. and Sergeant Lutz happened to answer. I couldn't help but mention the action of the man I'd told him about the day before, how he went to the Southfield P.D. with the intention of filing a report.

"That son of a bitch," said the Sergeant. "That son of a bitch."

"Yeah, it takes all kinds, huh?" I had the good Sergeant transfer my call and once again thought no more about the matter. Unbeknownst to me, however, Sergeant Lutz was becoming increasingly upset by the man who had had the audacity to mess with the department's favorite mouthpiece. And when he talked to several of the department's detectives about it, they became upset, too. So much so that they decided to pay the man a visit at his place of employment—a shoe store in the Northland Center mall. Just to have a talk.

The detectives waited in the parking lot by the man's

car around closing time and sure enough, the man came out. What he saw were four big guys in trench coats and fedoras standing beside his car. None of them identified themselves as police officers. One of them spoke.

"We understand you've got a little problem with one of our goombahs," the detective said, knowing the man was Italian and would most likely interpret the term in such a way as to suggest the detectives were anything but police officers. "We understand you threatened him. That's not something that exactly pleases us."

With that, all four detectives pulled their coats back to reveal their armament. These particular guys didn't travel light. Their weapon of choice was the .357 Magnum. The idea of course was just to throw a little scare into the man, mess with him a little. But the detectives had no idea how effective their plan would prove to be. Before another word was spoken, the man spun around and fled back to the confines of the mall.

None of the detectives had any interest in chasing him, of course. They stood in the parking lot laughing and figured their work was done. But to this day, nobody knows what became of the guy who threatened me in traffic on the access road off the freeway in Southfield, Michigan. All anybody knows for sure is that he never showed up for work at the shoe store again and that he never even came back for his car which eventually was impounded. Rumor has it that he took a bus out of town that very night. Apparently he had a brother in Santa Fe. But wherever he went, he was never seen again anywhere around the city of Detroit.

CHAPTER THIRTEEN

Appearances can be Deceiving

I'VE HAD CLIENTS FROM all walks of life and most of the time, what you see is what you get. But every now and again, you get a client who isn't at all what he or she appears to be. So it was with one James Carr. Carr established a brokerage in Boston, Massachusetts, to sell commodities futures—silver and gold mostly. Lloyd, Carr & Company was the name of the firm, although I never did learn who Lloyd was, if he even existed at all.

Carr's company relied on good old-fashioned telephone sales to drum up business. He'd get lists of potential investors from Dun & Bradstreet and he hired a roomful of salespeople to call them up. It was a textbook boiler room operation. The salespeople were given canned scripts and required to make at least a hundred calls a shift. It was apparently a two-call process, the sale of these futures. You'd call to qualify interest and ability, mail the prospect some brochures, and then make follow-up calls. The follow-up calls were strictly hard sell. The salespeople were trained to pester these people until they basically screamed uncle and invested in the futures.

Not surprisingly, there was a lot of turnover in the sales staff. But Carr made sure there were sales incentives and he worked hard, through his sales managers, to keep his people motivated. There were prizes including cash and appliances. Sales were celebrated by the ringing of bells. One manager dressed up in a gorilla suit and drove a moped around the floor to keep the sales force energized. But with the carrot, came the stick. Firings were routine. Sales quotas were strictly enforced. Once, during a period of unusually slow sales, a frustrated manager put everyone's name in a hat. Then he pulled several names out of the hat and fired them on the spot.

James Carr, meanwhile, was trying to do what he could to make things easier for the sales people. Unfortunately, that included allowing them to present information to prospective investors that wasn't exactly true. The canned sales pitches and the mailed information packets were—in strict legal terms—false, misleading, and deceptive. In less than legal terms, it was all a bunch of outright lies. Bullshit. Carr boasted a research department, for instance, with a one-million dollar annual budget. In reality, he had a few part-time employees doing research and they weren't doing it very well. Eighty-two percent of the investors lost money. The sales people were instructed to declare the exact opposite: eighty-two percent *made* money with Lloyd, Carr & Co. Risks were minimized and money received for investing was often just held by the company.

Carr was a scam artist, in other words. And a good one. His operation branched out, eventually encompassing eleven different offices around the country, each one a boiler room operation just like the original one he began in Boston. At one point he had a thousand employees working for him. All told, Carr would end up bilking investors out of twenty-eight million dollars, about eighty million in today's dollars. Meanwhile, he drove a Rolls Royce and lived in a waterfront mansion in Marblehead.

But that's not what I knew about him when he was referred to us for some legal help by the law firm of King and Spalding, a big, prestigious firm out of Atlanta that was founded back in 1885. All I knew was that James was looking to open a sales branch in Detroit but was having some problems with the phone company. Apparently they were skeptical of his business and reluctant to provide him a bunch of phones and phone service that could well be used to sell fraudulent securities. He assured us his business was strictly on the up and up and I had no reason to doubt him. We filed suit and prevailed. Over the next several months, we handled some other cases for James as well (he had a similar problem with the phone company in St. Louis, for example).

Once, George Bushnell and I flew to Boston to meet with James, and we were impressed by his operation there. James was a sharp guy, maybe the sharpest guy I'd ever met. I'd call him brilliant, in fact. Which was why George and I were so surprised when, meeting with James in his conference room, we heard a sudden disturbance out in the lobby where, upon further investigation, we observed no less than twenty FBI agents barreling their way into the offices of Lloyd, Carr, & Company.

"Whoa," said George to the guy who appeared to be leading the raid, "I'm Mr. Carr's attorney. What's the meaning of this?"

"It's a search, sir. I'd suggest you stand aside."

"Not until we see a search warrant." At this the agent produced the necessary warrant. George remained unconvinced. "I'm going to call the magistrate who supposedly issued this." But a quick phone call confirmed the warrant was valid.

"I'm sorry," I said, turning to James, "it looks like they have a legitimate ...." but James was gone. "James? Mr. Carr?"

George and I followed the agents down the corridor. Other agents were already tearing into the file cabinets. They took cash receipt books, purchase records, bank statements, sales material, account records, customer lists, and a pile of other material that would ultimately be used to prosecute Lloyd, Carr & Co. for fraud and a host of other violations. They prosecuted Carr and his managers. I don't know who represented Carr in court but it wasn't us. I never saw him again. When we walked back towards the conference room that day where we had last seen him, we noticed the door to the fire escape was open. Carr was gone.

Later we found out that James Carr wasn't James Carr at all. James was Alan Abrahams, an escaped felon. Don't ask me how he did it, but Abrahams had somehow managed to get licensed as a commodities broker with the Commodities Futures Trading Commission under the name of James Carr. The licensing process supposedly includes an FBI background check. The same law enforcement agency that burst through the doors of Lloyd, Carr that day could have saved themselves the trouble a year or so earlier by discovering that James Carr was not only a convicted felon: he was a convicted felon who was on the run having escaped four years earlier from a New Jersey prison farm where he'd been serving a six-year sentence for—what else?—fraud.

Anyway, according to the news reports I read later, they found Abrahams not very far away from his office the day of the search. They arrested him, took his fingerprints, and then he was released on $100,000 bond. That's when he skipped out again. In the meantime, a fingerprint search revealed his true identity. Months later, Abrahams was found in Florida where he had dyed his hair and had been living with his family under yet another assumed name. He'd been characterized, incidentally, as "armed and dangerous."

Alan Abrahams ended up changing the procedure for certification of commodities brokers. From that point on, getting fingerprinted became part of the background check.

Had they cross-checked Carr's fingerprints originally, prior to the establishment of Lloyd, Carr & Co., they would have discovered he was Abrahams and saved the public close to thirty million bucks.

As for us, we got bilked, too. Not surprisingly, our invoice to Lloyd, Carr & Co. for legal services rendered went unpaid.

〜

Sometimes when you discover that a client isn't what he or she appears to be, it's a good thing. Like the shoplifter I represented who, it turns out, wasn't a shoplifter after all. She was a doctor. A pediatrician from Ohio. But shopping in a T.J. Maxx one day she ended up being arrested for stealing some crystal. Charged with theft, she sought the help of an attorney who advised her to plead guilty. "But won't they take my state medical license?" she said. The attorney assured her they wouldn't. So she pleaded guilty. And the state promptly took her medical license. That's when she came to me.

Obviously the woman had been improperly represented. I decided to try to get her conviction overturned. And after listening to her story, I knew I could do it. The facts of the case were roughly these: the woman had been pushing a shopping cart through the T.J. Maxx in question when she decided to purchase a couple of crystal wine glasses she came upon. She put the glasses in her cart and continued to make her way around the store. The problem was that the glasses were rattling in her cart, clinking against each other and making the woman concerned that they would chip or even break. So she put them in her purse where they were more secure and she continued shopping, ultimately buying several items. Unfortunately, she forgot about the crystal glasses. And when she got outside of the store, a female security guard stopped her, searched her purse, and had her arrested. My client, of course, was extremely apologetic and tried to explain how the glasses ended up in her purse, but the overzealous security guard was having none of it.

At the retrial, I brought an actual shopping cart into the courtroom. I placed two crystal wine glasses into it and pushed it around the floor so the jury could hear the clinking. "My client's actions certainly seem perfectly reasonable," I said. "And after a lot more shopping in the store, she made the perfectly human mistake of forgetting about the glasses. This woman," I continued, pointing at my client, "is certainly no thief. She's a well-respected pediatrician."

Every juror but one agreed with me. The twelfth held out for a time, but eventually she, too, would concede the taking of the glasses was an innocent mistake. Did she really believe it? I'll never know. My understanding from one of the other jurors was that she wanted to get on with the verdict because she didn't want to miss a hair appointment. Sometimes timing is everything.

But then for all the trouble my client had gone through, we decided there was a cause of action against T.J. Maxx for the overzealousness of that security guard. We sued. And researching the case, I discovered other cases of overzealousness by that same guard. There was one case in particular that stood out and I decided to seize on it.

"Miss Smith," I said when I ultimately got the security guard on the stand during our false arrest lawsuit, "my client isn't the first person you've had wrongfully arrested, is she?"

"I don't know what you're referring to," the guard said.

"Well, do you remember the case of a certain man you tried to have arrested for stealing women's shoes one day last year?"

"Well, yes ... there might have been someone ...."

"The fact is that you stopped a man after he left your store last February and you accused him of having shoved a shoe down the front of his pants for the purpose of smuggling it out of the store, is that correct?"

"Well, yes. The man had been hanging around the women's shoe department. He seemed ... suspicious."

"I see. So when you stopped him, did he indeed have a shoe down the front of his pants?"

"No."

"But you thought you saw something there, didn't you?"

"Yes."

"And could you please tell the jury what it was he really had under his pants that day?"

The security guard mumbled something.

"I'm sorry," I said, "Could you please repeat that for the court?"

"An erection."

"An erection?"

"Yes. He had an erection."

"And just so we understand, you mistook the man's erection for a shoe? Is that correct?"

"Well, I ... I ... it looked like it could have been a shoe!" she blurted out at last, completely red-faced.

"No further questions," I said.

T.J. Maxx and my client ultimately settled.

Looking back at that case, I feel very fortunate to have won it. Not just because of the previous instance of false accusation against the man with the apparent shoe fetish, but because the pediatrician was of Iranian descent. The case was in November of 1979, two weeks before Iranian revolutionary students, under the leadership of the Ayatollah Khomeini, took over the United States embassy and held fifty-two Americans hostage. Iran was suddenly public enemy number one.

I remember "Fuck Iran" t-shirts and buttons and caps. It was a pretty ugly mood around the country and I can't imagine the difficulties in trying to assemble a jury full of people who wouldn't harbor at least some animosity towards an Iranian. Had the trial taken place just a couple weeks later, we might well have had a different outcome. Just like with the juror's hair appointment, sometimes timing is everything.

There's an old saying often attributed to Freud that sometimes a cigar is just a cigar. But sometimes, a successful commodities trader can be an escaped felon and sometimes an Iranian shoplifter can be a well-respected law-abiding pediatrician. And sometimes, a shoe can even be an erection. It's a strange world.

CHAPTER FOURTEEN

David v. Goliath

WOULD YOU RATHER be represented by twenty attorneys or only two? Before you answer, you might want to consider the case of *Martin v. the Fortune 500 Company* or, as I like to call it, *David v. Goliath*.

Joe Martin was a salesman for the Detroit branch of a large, highly-respected office supply company. He was personable and ambitious and very successful. He was also African-American and what Joe began to realize over time was that when it came time for the branch manager to dole out bonuses, he wasn't getting any. The other guys in the office—white guys every one—were the ones getting the bonuses. And Joe got passed over for a couple promotions, too, and was once even given an unfair job evaluation in direct contradiction to the facts, which were that Joe was doing a very effective job.

Joe complained to the manager who said he didn't want to hear about it and if Joe really wanted to pursue the matter, he could take it up the ladder in accord with the company protocol. Joe did just that, filing a grievance with a regional manager who reviewed the grievance and found it to be "without merit." Joe appealed, all the way to the company CEO in New York, a guy we'll call Mr. Alan. Mr. Alan supposedly had what he called an "open door policy." This meant that if an employee had a beef against the company, that employee, no matter how low on the totem pole, could bring said beef to the attention of the very top man. But when Mr. Alan was presented with Joe's grievance, it was more or less in the form of a one-paragraph summary that his assistant typed up for him to review. The summary essentially confirmed the regional manager's position that the grievance was without merit and Mr. Alan signed off on it. He didn't actually read the grievance; he didn't read the investigative report that went with it; and he didn't read the internal analysis that went with the investigative report. He read a few lines his assistant put together. So much for his policy of openness.

In any event, Joe received a perfunctory letter back from Mr. Alan dismissing his complaint. Joe was left with no choice but to leave the company and eventually he got in touch with me. I did some preliminary research and discovered a pattern of discrimination with the company in question. Joe had a case and we filed suit.

It was during my deposition of Mr. Alan in New York that I discovered what his real process of grievance review was like. The deposition was what's known as an apex deposition—a deposition of a top-level executive. The theory is that in a company with thousands of employees, with lots of possibilities for lawsuits, frivolous or otherwise, a top executive could easily get bogged down doing nothing but attending depositions. To secure an apex deposition, you have to show that the executive in question—Mr. Alan in our case—had superior knowledge of the circumstances. Without a direct connection to the events of the case, the executive can't be deposed and you have to settle for an underling. In this case, with Mr. Alan's openness policy, we could show that connection. Presumably, he'd received Joe Martin's complaint personally.

Or had he? When I questioned him, he hemmed and

hawed about the exact amount of depth he personally went into with any given complaint sent to his office. I kept badgering him for the truth, which wasn't easy to get out of him.

"You seem to be implying that I am some sort of liar," he huffed at one point.

"Sir, if the shoe fits," I replied. "Isn't this the truth, Mr. Alan? Isn't the truth that your process of 'openness' is not much more than a cursory glance at your assistant's summary?" He had to confess that it was. From that point, the rest of the deposition pretty much belonged to me.

Meanwhile, I ordered a trial subpoena for Mr. Alan. I couldn't wait to get him on the stand in Detroit. Alan's salary was $5 million a year. I knew that the average salary of a typical Detroit juror at the time was about eighty bucks a week.

Eventually, the case came to trial. At the plaintiff's table there was my second wife Ivy and me. By then, Ivy had become a partner in my firm and she took an active role in Joe's case. The office equipment company, meanwhile, had hired the largest law firm in Michigan for their defense. Plus they brought along their own in-house lawyers. There were a couple of them at the defense table but an entire army of them at the back of the courtroom. All told, the company had twenty attorneys representing them. This was fine by me and for a couple reasons. First, you don't call in that much support unless you're worried. The company must have known their case was on thin ice. Second, I knew that representation by committee could be problematic for the same reason that doing anything by committee can be problematic. Too many chefs, goes the saying. I knew these guys would be stepping all over themselves.

I also used their size to my advantage when I interviewed the jurors. One of my questions was this: "Is there any among you who personally knows any one of the *multitude* of attorneys that the defense has seen fit to bring in here this morning?" I was outmanned and I wanted the jurors to know it. Everybody loves an underdog.

In the jury selection process, I was shooting for an African-American majority. The company exercised peremptory challenges. You're allowed to reject a certain number of jurors without stating a reason. But there's an exception to this. In the precedent-setting case of *Batson v. Kentucky*, it was held that you can't dismiss a juror on the basis of race. If race is an issue, in other words, you'd better have a good reason for rejecting a juror. So I invoked what's become known as the Batson challenge, forcing the defendant's hand. I made them state their reasons and they couldn't come up with credible ones for why they were rejecting the black jurors ("I didn't like the look he gave me," was a reason given for the rejection of one particular jury candidate). It didn't hurt our side that the judge listening to their arguments was an African-American woman. And she could see right through the defense's strategy leaving her no choice but to declare a mistrial.

Now, this was actually viewed as good news for the company. With the glacier-like pace of the court system, they figured they'd have months, maybe even a year, before a new trial would convene. But that hope was quickly squelched by the judge who informed both sides that a new jury would be called the very next day. I glanced over at the defense table and you could see the look of alarm on their faces.

The next day came and the company, cognizant of how a challenge to any given juror would look to the judge and knowing I was ready to wield Batson as the situation called for it, produced very little opposition to my selections, and I was able to get the African-American majority I'd wanted. By this time, Court TV had gotten wind of the case and when the trial got underway, the cameras began to roll, much to the dismay of the company.

My first witness was the branch manager. I started denting his credibility immediately with questions about his background. Turns out his self-proclaimed bachelor's degree was actually a two-year associate's degree. A small matter, maybe, in the greater scheme of things, but enough to get the jury to question everything he said from that point forward.

And then I began to ask him about the chain of command at the company. There was the regional head, he explained, and then a series of lesser positions until you got down to the territorial salespeople. As he explained each position, I decided to help him illustrate the chain by writing the names of the people who held each position in Joe Martin's region on a large drawing board at the front of the courtroom. With a black magic marker, I wrote the names from left to right across the page, finally writing in Joe's name at the far right side.

"Is this a fair representation, then," I asked, "of the chain of command in this region of the organization?" The manager allowed that it was. Then I took the marker and drew the outline of a bus around the names, with the regional head representing the driver of the bus. I drew wheels on it and everything. I'm not an artist but I thought it looked pretty good.

"So you're saying, sir," I then said, "that—essentially—Joe Martin is being made to ride in the back of the bus?" I could hear snickering from the jury box and even saw the slightest trace of a smile cross the judge's face.

Later that night I got a call from the company's top in-house attorney. I can't say it was unexpected. "Noel," he said, "we'd like to settle." I said sure and gave him a number. He gasped. Then he accepted it. "Deal," he said.

I'd find out later that the attorney had been instructed to settle the case at any price and so I probably left some money on the table; but the amount we received was more than I had hoped for and certainly more than Joe was expecting. He was so thrilled that to celebrate, he ran out, rented a Rolls Royce, drove to his old branch office, and parked outside, laying on the horn until the manager came out. Then he threw the manager a wave and took off.

CHAPTER FIFTEEN

My Picasso

AS IT TURNS OUT, there was one little hitch before Joe Martin was able to celebrate with that Rolls Royce. What Joe hadn't told me was that after he'd left the office supply company, and before the trial and subsequent settlement, his financial situation had grown so dire that he found himself forced to declare personal bankruptcy. His debts were in the neighborhood of $40,000. This was a fact he held off sharing with me until the settlement was official.

"Joe," I said, "I sure wish you had told me that earlier. Your bankruptcy trustee now has a claim to the settlement proceeds. We're going to need to go through him before we can do anything." Joe said he understood and left it to me to make contact with the bankruptcy trustee, which I did, telling him that Joe had come into a rather large amount of money in a court settlement and that he was ready and able to pay off his creditors, with interest, as well as pay the trustee's fee, whatever that might be. And that's where we came across the little hitch.

"Just how much is the settlement?" asked the trustee.

"Well," I explained, "I'm afraid I can't say. Part of the deal was that the settlement remain sealed and so I remain under a court order not to disclose the amount." I assumed that would be that, but what the trustee said next took me aback.

"Listen," he said, "I don't really give a crap about your

court order. The settlement amount has to go through me. Your client is bankrupt. For all intents and purposes, that money belongs to me, as trustee. Now, I need to know how much the amount is, so I will ask you again: how much was the settlement for?"

"And I'll answer again," I said. "I cannot disclose the amount. I'm under a court order and could be held in contempt." I repeated the part about being willing to pay the creditors with interest as well as pay the trustee's fee, but the trustee reiterated his position that he needed to know the amount and then said something about getting it out of me one way or another before hanging up.

Two days later I received a subpoena to appear in bankruptcy court to testify about the amount of Joe's settlement. This time, I was being asked by a bankruptcy court judge. But my answer had to be the same.

"Your Honor," I said, "I risk a contempt charge if I divulge an amount that is sealed under a court order."

"Mr. Gage," the judge said, "you risk a contempt order in this court if you do *not* divulge the amount." I sat quietly, pondering the rock and the hard place between which I had been suddenly placed. "Tell you what," the judge said finally, pointing to me and the trustee, "why don't you two figure out a way to hammer this out and we'll reconvene in two weeks."

Bankruptcy court was obviously new to me. A fool hires himself as a lawyer, they say, and so I met with a bankruptcy attorney. I explained my predicament while he listened intently, telling him all about the court order that I remain silent on the amount of Joe's settlement.

He nodded, understandingly. Then he said, "So how much was the amount?"

"I can't say!" I replied, incredulously. "That's my point.

That's why I'm here!"

"But you can tell me. I'm your lawyer."

By then, I'd gotten a pretty good idea of how bankruptcy court works. It's a small club. The judge no doubt knew the trustee and I'm sure the attorney I was consulting with knew them both. There was no doubt in my mind that my secret wouldn't stay secret for long. And I started putting something else together. These guys—the lawyer and the trustee—were waiting until they learned the amount before determining their fees. Just how much was Joe worth now? That was the burning issue. Months later, I would learn my suspicions were correct: in fact, the trustee's typical fee was three percent of whatever he could wrangle from a debtor. It was like a commission. And three percent of Joe's settlement would have been a small fortune for a bankruptcy trustee. The lawyer, of course, could smell money, too. Just how much could he get out of me?

Though I didn't know all that at the time, I still didn't feel comfortable disclosing the settlement amount to the attorney, even if he *was* going to be my lawyer.

"You're not my lawyer yet," I replied. "And I won't tell you."

"Then I'm not sure I can represent you."

"Then don't," I said and I walked out of his office.

Two weeks later I was in front of the judge again.

"Look, Your Honor, I might not know much about bankruptcy court but I remember back from my days in law school that the appeal from here is to a federal district court judge. So let me go there. Stay the proceedings and let's see what the federal judge says. If he says I need to disclose the amount of my client's settlement, then I'll assume his ruling takes priority over the state order and I'll reveal the amount. But only then."

Fortunately, the judge seemed to think that was a fair enough way to proceed and he let me leave, satisfied with the idea of allowing the issue to be appealed to the Federal District Court judge. I went home and called Joe to fill him in on the details, telling him how adamant the trustee was that we disclose the amount Joe was getting from the office equipment company. Joe was livid.

"That's none of his goddamn business!" he said. "And why doesn't the judge tell him so?"

"I don't know, Joe," I said. "The nearest I can figure is that they know each other too well. The bankruptcy world is a small one. I just feel lucky that the judge stayed the proceedings for now."

"But I need to get this settled," said Joe. "I need that money."

"I know, Joe. I know."

"Well, maybe there's something I can do," said Joe and he hung up, leaving me wondering what he had in mind. Later that day, I wondered no longer. The bankruptcy trustee was on the phone to me.

"Hey, Gage," he said, "your client is out front of my office with about ten of his buddies and they're all carrying signs saying I'm a racist. I can't even get to my car!"

"You don't say."

"Yeah, and I just got a call from the judge. Your guy has a bunch of people marching around in front of his office, too! There are TV cameras down there and everything. He just called me pissed as hell. Told me we need to settle this case now. So let's settle and you can tell your guy to back off."

"Settle?" I said. "What do you think I've been trying to do?!"

So anyway, the trustee and I came to an agreement on an appropriate fee—way less than what would have been three percent of Joe's settlement—and Joe was able to secure his money, pay everybody off, with interest, and still have enough left over to look like a guy who could buy a Rolls Royce. For my part, I vowed never to go to bankruptcy court again.

But my dealings with the Fortune 500 office equipment company didn't end there. It turns out I was just getting started, and in ways I could not have anticipated. Other employees of theirs started coming to me. In a relatively short period of time, I had eleven more discrimination suits against the company. That prompted the head attorney to contact me once again. "Let's settle them all," he said. And then he said something else, something I wasn't at all expecting. "And after we're done settling, we'd like to hire you." I guess I'd sufficiently impressed them and they must have figured that the best way to get rid of me as a thorn in their side was to bring me aboard.

"Well," I said, "I can't really do that. It's really not ethical for me to advise my clients to settle with a company that's considering employing my services." He said he understood and took the matter back to the company. So intent were they on hiring me that they consulted with a well-known professor of ethics at Yale Law School, looking for a way around the ethical conundrum their offer to me presented. The professor reasoned that everything would be perfectly ethical if all eleven of my clients were informed of the job offer and gave their express consent to settling their cases knowing I'd be subsequently hired by the company.

Well, that was good enough for me and it was good enough for the clients as well. The settlements were huge and immediate. Afterwards, I was made national trial counsel for the company, a position I held for ten years. My function was to train their in-house lawyers and defend the company from time to time in various lawsuits. I was given a sizable retainer and paid extra for work that went beyond what was expected.

The company was generous with expenses, too. One time I found out just how generous. I was living in El Paso and I had agreed to fly to Amarillo to take a deposition for the company. Not a lot of air traffic came in or out of Amarillo in those days. During the deposition, the opposing counsel, knowing my questioning of his client was slowly destroying his case, resolved to get a little revenge by extending the proceedings as long as possible, past 5:00 p.m. which, as it happened, was the time of the last flight out of town. By the time we finished, the last plane was long gone.

The problem was that I had been fighting the flu and had a temperature of 103 degrees. I needed to get home. Or at least I needed a decent hotel. But there were no decent hotels in Amarillo at the time and I couldn't even find an indecent one. There were no decent restaurants, either. "I'm getting home some way," I said to the opposing counsel as we walked out into the street. "I'm going to the airport."

"Hell, I'll take you there," he said. "Good luck getting on a plane, though. And there ain't no place to sleep in the airport, either, and no place to eat. But if you want to go, I'll be tickled to take you."

"Just get me there," I said. "I'll find a way home." So the man drove me to the airport, chuckling to himself the whole way.

"Good luck!" he said, laughing, as he let me out of the car.

True to his word, there were no more planes flying anywhere, the first one back to El Paso leaving around noon the next day. With no other choice, I decided, at my own expense, to charter a plane. There was a Twin Beech, a propeller plane, available for charter and the pilot got me to El Paso later that night. I went home and fell into bed. I called the head attorney the next morning to let him know how the deposition went and I happened to mention the plane.

"Noel," he said, "why didn't you charter a jet?"

"A jet?" I said. "Well, that can be a little pricey."

"So what? We're paying for it. Next time, do yourself a favor and get yourself a jet." In the meantime, he made sure I was reimbursed for the cost of the Twin Beech charter, an expense I had just assumed would be mine. I never took advantage of the company's generosity, but it sure was nice knowing that I could charter a jet plane anytime I felt as though I needed one.

All in all, the company turned out to be okay. I know for a fact that their discrimination practices stopped, and I'd like to think I made the place a little better for my efforts. I can't do the work of twenty attorneys, of course. But then again, maybe that's not such a bad thing.

And I think Joe Martin, for one, would agree. A few months after our trial, he invited me to drop by his new house. He had a piece of artwork he wanted to show me. I couldn't imagine what he'd purchased with the settlement money. A Renoir? A van Gogh? To Joe it was something even better. There it was, hanging on his living room wall in a gold frame.

"*That*," Joe said, pointing up at it, "is my Picasso."

It wasn't really a Picasso. What Joe meant was that the artwork, if you can call it that, was worth as much to him as any Picasso could possibly be worth. I laughed when I recognized the handiwork. Joe had managed to retrieve from the courtroom my crude drawing of the metaphorical office equipment company bus that I had presented to the jury during our trial. There it was, hanging in all its glory on his wall. I have to confess it looked pretty good in that gold frame.

CHAPTER SIXTEEN

West Texas Town of El Paso

WHEN I VENTURED DOWN to Texas with Ed Ritenour to confront the unscrupulous chiropractor, it was not a one-time event. I'd been sent down there before by the automobile manufacturer to review a particular Texas-based case. The company had legal representation in El Paso, but they were having reservations about the firm they had hired and they wanted me to check out the firm and report back. As one might expect, the El Paso guys weren't too keen on having a stranger come in and review their case files. But the manufacturer insisted and so they had little choice. What I found was bad news for the El Paso firm. I could tell right away that they didn't have the level of expertise needed to defend the manufacturer properly. I reported what I'd found, and at that point the manufacturer asked me to handle the Texas cases, of which there were quite a few.

The problem was that I wasn't licensed to practice law in Texas and there was no reciprocity between Texas and Michigan. I had to take a bar exam. I passed, with a score of exactly one-hundred percent, but that didn't mean I could start practicing law right away. Texas at the time was leery of outsiders coming into their state—carpetbaggers from the North, if you will. And so my license was delayed. No reason was ever given but the paperwork somehow just kept slipping through the cracks. Weeks went by. Fortunately, Hilda had a friend in Texas who was a powerful judge. Sometimes it pays to know the right people. One phone call on a Friday and I had my Texas law license the following Monday.

It turned out that the manufacturer had enough cases in Texas that I felt it was worth opening a branch office there. In time, I would move there with my second wife, Ivy, settling in El Paso where we would live for eight years. My partners there included James Kennedy and Timothy Harrington, superb lawyers. James spoke fluent Spanish which was invaluable. He also happened to be a passionate fisherman, regularly participating in fishing tournaments around the world, including an annual marlin tournament in Cabo San Lucas that bills itself as the richest tournament anywhere. The entry fee runs upwards of ten grand and the prizes are routinely over a million dollars. Both James and Timothy were excellent trial attorneys who could wow juries. Most important, both always put their clients first.

I liked El Paso. The people were warm and friendly. There was only one time, outside a courtroom, that I really had a disagreement with anyone. A local office supply store sold my office a copy machine that failed to function properly. This was back in the days when copy machines could be rather pricey. Two weeks after our purchase, the machine started having problems. Repair guys would come and go but nobody could keep the machine working for very long. I requested a new one, a request I thought was more than reasonable given the expense of the machine and its failure to perform.

The office supply store refused. Soon they even stopped taking my calls. My office was adjacent to a major highway. I rented a crane, hoisted the machine up to where cars passing by on the highway could see it, and I put a sign on top that said "Lemon" and the name of the store. The local paper even printed a picture. The store provided a new machine two days later.

It was a strategy I'd used once before, in Detroit, but on a slightly pricier product. Less than a year after having purchased a brand-new Mercedes Benz, the car somehow caught fire as I was driving it. Smoke started pouring out from under the hood. I called the dealership.

"You'll find your car on the side of the road," I said, telling them where I'd left it. "Naturally, I expect a new one to replace it." The dealership balked.

"It's a year old," the manager said.

"But it caught fire," I replied. "Putting my life in danger. How can you sell a car that can't go a year without catching fire? This thing was obviously defective from the start."

"I'm sorry," he said. "We can't replace the car with a new one."

"Okay. Then I'm afraid you've given me little choice. Do you know Telegraph Road?" The manager said he did. Telegraph Road was a major thoroughfare. "And do you know the Farmer Jack store on the corner of Michigan Avenue?" Another main thoroughfare. "Tomorrow I'm going to have your burned out car towed to that corner and I'm going to put a basket of lemons on top with a sign saying courtesy of your dealership. And then I'm going to invite all the local television stations."

I got my new car.

⤻

El Paso is about an hour's drive from Las Cruces, New Mexico, home of New Mexico State University. We took a case from there once that I would never forget. I wasn't licensed to practice in New Mexico, but James Kennedy was and when he found himself tied up with another case, he dished this one to me.

It seems an attractive coed had been out at a hotel bar having a couple drinks with her boyfriend. Sometime after midnight, she excused herself to use the restroom which was down the hotel corridor. As she walked out of the bar and down the corridor, she noticed two men standing in an alcove by a side exit door. Both were looking at her and laughing. The woman used the restroom whereupon, returning to the bar, she passed the two men again who were now laughing harder. She tried to ignore them as she walked past them. But suddenly they reached out and grabbed her.

The woman struggled and it took the men at least two full minutes to pull her outside through the side door. The timing would become important. After they got her outside of the hotel, they threw her into their car and took off for the desert where, in a lonely secluded spot, they raped and sodomized her for two full hours. Then they left her naked in the dark. Seeing a light in the distance, she hiked towards it, eventually making her way to a house where the home-owner called the police.

While the criminal investigation dragged on, the woman determined that she had a cause of action against the hotel. For as it happened, watching the abduction the whole time, was a hotel maintenance worker with a walkie-talkie. The problem was he didn't use it. Not until the woman was already in the parking lot being shoved into the car. Two precious minutes went by before the worker had the presence of mind to raise the front desk on his walkie-talkie so that the police could be called. Of course by then, the men and their captive were long gone.

We sued the hotel, asking for a million dollars in damages. When I met with the woman I found her smart and articulate. We had two problems as far as I could see. Las Cruces was a very conservative town. Although it was objectively wrong to do so, I knew the jurors might question the woman's credibility simply on account of her tattoos, which covered her entire body. Second, a million-dollar verdict—justified as far as I was concerned—would have been a record for the city of Las Cruces at that time. The average annual income of the jurors was probably around $15,000. Were we asking for too much? Would the jury be willing to award an amount none of them would ever see in their lifetimes?

"You'll need to cover those tattoos," I told my client, noting the conservative climate of the town. "Dark stockings, long-sleeve shirt."

"Guess I better not wear a midriff then, huh?" she said.

"Why's that?"

"Because of this one." And then the woman raised her blouse to reveal the tattoo of an arrow on her stomach, pointing downwards.

"Yep. Better not wear a midriff."

Tattoos or no tattoos, the client made a great witness, just as smart and articulate on the stand as she'd been with me before the trial. As I made my closing statement, I sensed we had the case in the bag. I asked the jury for a million but told them there was nothing to keep them from awarding more. "That's just a suggestion," I said.

I guess the defense thought we had the case won, too, because when the jury went back to deliberate, the defense attorney offered to settle. For $950,000. A million had a much nicer ring to it, but we took the offer. The rapists were never found. But the woman took a large portion of the settlement and made a generous donation to a local woman's shelter. The people running the shelter were thrilled and when the word got out, my client was interviewed on the local news. I happened to catch the broadcast. She wore a short-sleeve blouse and she looked just fine to me, tattoos and all. But I did notice she kept her midsection covered.

꙳

Another unforgettable experience during my time in El Paso involved a rather odd West Texas judge. I'd met some strange judges in my time as a lawyer, but this guy might have been the strangest. Three hours to the east of El Paso is the town of Odessa, which happened to be where the only federal judge in the area was located. I had a federal case and found myself before this odd judge. His major hang-up—I imagine there were probably several—was that he detested lawyers approaching the witness stand.

Now, most judges want to control the courtroom and they dislike it when an attorney just sort of saunters around wherever he pleases as he's doing his examination or cross-examination. Plus, an attorney can be more intimidating if he gets right in the face of a witness, which of course judges want to avoid in the interest of fairness. So even though you see TV and movie attorneys constantly placing themselves within inches of the witness stand, in a real life federal court-room, you always have to ask for permission to approach. Normally it's readily granted, but you still have to ask. And although it's understandable for a judge to not want to con-cede the floor of his courtroom to the whims of an attorney, this Odessa judge took his authority just a little too far.

Not that he was going to be the first judge I'd come across to have a fixation on attorneys approaching witnesses. One time in Detroit, in perhaps the largest courtroom in the courthouse, I had approached a doctor on the stand so that he could see a certain exhibit. I asked and was granted per-mission to do so. Then I walked back to the defense table to pick up another exhibit and turned and stepped back towards the doctor again. At this point, the judge abruptly excused the jury. Nobody knew why until the jury had gone and then it became clear. The judge was intent on ruthlessly berating me in front of my client.

"Mr. Gage!" he boomed. "You are *never* to approach a witness without my permission! Is this your first trial?!"

"I ... I'm sorry, Your Honor, but I have an exhibit here to show the witness. You had already given your permission—."

"That was *before*, Mr. Gage! I had given you permission for that one question about that one particular exhibit. That is all I will allow you to approach, sir!" Then he yelled a few more things at me, all of which were surprising in their own right, but more so because the judge happened to be acquainted with my wife. Hilda had become something of a legal scholar by then and the judge had often prevailed upon her for her expertise on case law. I had gotten to know the man outside of the courtroom. We weren't friends, exactly, but it wasn't as if I was a complete stranger coming into his courtroom to blatantly flout the rules.

Finally, after his barrage, the jury was summoned back in and I collected myself and continued my examination of the witness.

"Doctor," I began, standing behind the lectern which was a good fifteen feet from the witness stand, "Can you please tell the jury if this is, indeed, your signature on the bottom of this document." The document I held up was a medical form printed with an extremely small font, and the signature line at the very bottom allowed for maybe an eighth-inch space into which the doctor had squeezed his signature. It was hard to see even up close.

"I'm sorry, Mr. Gage," the doctor said, squinting and craning his neck forward. "I'm afraid I can't make that out from here."

"Well, I'm sorry, Doctor, but His Honor has ordered that I must show you the document from where I am standing. Can you please try harder?"

This produced a tittering from the courtroom, notably from the jury box, and the judge was forced to concede the necessity of my approaching the witness.

"You may approach, counselor," he grumbled.

I don't think the exchange had a real bearing on the outcome, but the jury was out for only eighteen minutes before rendering a decision in our favor, a personal record for me. A couple weeks later, I saw the judge in a grocery store and I couldn't resist. On neutral turf, outside of his domain, I gave him an earful about humiliating me in front of my client for no good reason. He shrugged and pushed his cart along.

In the Odessa case, the federal judge would allow you to approach any given witness but only just once. Even if you asked. After the first time, he had a very unusual way of conveying his disapproval and it was more than just a strong verbal rebuke like what I had received in Detroit. But I had done my homework, so I knew all about the judge and his peculiar manner of admonishment. My worthy opponent, however, had no idea. And so, after having already approached a particular witness, my opponent began to approach for a second time, asking permission *while* walking towards the witness stand.

"Permission to approach," he said, obviously assuming it would be automatically granted, as would be typical in most courtrooms. But this was not most courtrooms. As the unsuspecting attorney continued towards the stand, the judge reached under his desk and pulled out a large water gun. It was of the "Super Soaker" variety of toy water weapons which meant the gun had a small tank of water attached to it and the stream of water was enhanced by manually pressurized air. The attorney never stood a chance. Within seconds he was drenched.

"Permission to approach denied," the judge said.

I'm pretty sure I won the case, but it's hard to remember any of the details outside of a strange judge with a powerful water gun spraying a poor unsuspecting Texas attorney. Oh, I do remember one other thing: the attorney never approached a witness again for the duration of the trial.

⤳

In El Paso, I met the man I consider to be the best medical malpractice lawyer in the country, though the introduction got off to a less than friendly start. Rockne Onstad came from Austin for a deposition, called in to help an El Paso attorney who represented the opposing side of a case I was involved in. Rockne, or Rock as I would come to know him, was a former Marine captain, a Vietnam vet, and a Texan through and through. He sauntered into my pristine boardroom where the witness to be deposed was waiting, sat down across from me, leaned back, and proceeded to rest his dirty cowboy boots up on the table.

"Let's get started," he said.

I was always thorough in my questioning, but Rock was at least as thorough. The deposition took close to eight hours. And it was contentious throughout, both sides objecting to questions and objecting often. When it ended, Rock called me a prick. But I guess I was a prick he could respect because he remembered me whenever he had a case he thought I could help him with, and I did the same. Rock, without a medical degree, nevertheless knew much more about medicine than I, and more, I suspect, than most physicians. His skill in cross-examining witnesses, especially doctors, was fun to watch. In time, we became great friends. Rock still runs a highly successful practice in Austin.

Meanwhile, I split with the New York firm, Herzfeld and Rubin, that we had worked with when we were handling the Michigan and Texas automobile product liability cases. The split with New York was an amicable one over honest differences. They wanted me to focus exclusively on the defense of product liability cases. But I was still taking on quite a few plaintiff cases. Frankly, those cases paid better. I frequently took more satisfaction in them, too. Often I'd have a client who was legitimately harmed in some manner but who had no way, other than through my efforts, to fight some behemoth corporation with deep pockets whose negligence was responsible for the client's injuries. It's a good feeling when you win a case or negotiate a large settlement for someone who otherwise wouldn't stand a chance at procuring any kind of redress. And so in a meeting one day on Wall Street, the New York firm and I decided to go our separate ways.

Of course, many of the plaintiff cases I continued to focus on required the creativity and inventive solutions that I'd become known for. Interestingly enough, while in Texas, I had to use some of that creativity against my old partners from New York who were defending the manufacturer. The case involved the crash of a pickup truck full of Hispanic teenagers.

Three boys and three girls were out for a night of fun. They were joy-riding, as kids are wont to do. It started as one boy with his girlfriend. He'd borrowed the truck from his dad and picked up his girl and they'd driven to the local teen hotspot, a burger and shake joint. There, they'd met up with two other couples and the six had all piled into the front seat of the truck and decided to take a spin around town. There was no alcohol involved or drugs; it was just six kids out for a joyride. And all were badly hurt when the young man driving the truck lost control and the truck slammed into a viaduct.

I filed suit against the manufacturer who was represented by my old firm. Truthfully, I wasn't at all sure I had a case. The truck had been traveling at a high rate of speed and having six people in the cab was obviously unsafe to begin with. In fact, the manufacturer had put a notice in plain sight on the dashboard stating that no more than three people should ever ride in the cab of the truck. But I felt sick about the result of the accident and when the parents of one of the kids came to see me, I promised I'd see what I could do.

One of my old partners called and tried to talk me out of the case.

"Noel," he said, "I know how knowledgeable and capable you are with automotive product liability cases. Hell, I know it because we're the ones who trained you. So you must be able to see that you have no case here."

And just then, an idea hit me.

"Well," I replied, "I'm not so sure. I can show a lot of the injuries, and maybe even the loss of control itself, can be pinned to the fact that there were six people in the cab."

"Yeah? So?"

"So I think we have a legitimate failure to warn case on our hands."

"But, Noel, you're forgetting the notice on the dash. 'No more than three occupants.'"

"Well, the thing about the notice is that it's in English."

"Of course."

"But my clients are Hispanic. And they only speak Spanish."

There was a long pause and then my old partner finally said, "Oh, c'mon, Noel."

"I have to tell you," I said, "I like my chances." Now, whether or not I had a really good case, I don't know. But I could tell by that pause that my old partner was suddenly very concerned. And not only that, he knew I was not only capable, but I was also just crazy enough to go through with the failure to warn suit. He said something about talking it over with the client and I got a call later that day with an offer to settle that was even more than I'd hoped for.

Now, although I can't exactly connect it, I started noticing from that time forward that a lot of manufacturer warning stickers and labels were suddenly showing up in both English and Spanish. I'm sure it's coincidence, but it's fun to think that maybe word somehow got out about a new legal strategy whereby manufacturers could be sued for not using bilingual warnings about the dangers of their products.

～

I saved perhaps my most creative solution for a motorcycle manufacturer. An El Paso man came to me one day with huge medical bills from a bike accident. There was no way he could even begin to pay them.

"Can you do anything for me?" he asked pleadingly. Truthfully, I didn't see how I could. The fault was clearly his. Out riding his motorcycle one fine morning, the man had absent-mindedly ridden right through a red light, t-boning a car. The man flew over the handlebars of the bike and then over the car, landing in a broken heap in the middle of the road. He had several broken bones and had spent weeks in the hospital. Now he owed a small fortune. But the circumstances certainly seemed open and shut. I was about to tell him he didn't have even a scintilla of a case, but there was a quiet desperation in the guy's eyes that I decided

I could not ignore.

"Okay," I said. "Let me think about it and see what I can do." He left my office, leaving behind some photographs of the wrecked motorcycle. Later that day, an idea hit me and I called the man back.

"We're filing suit," I said.

"Great! What made you decide?"

"Your photographs," I said. "Why, I notice that there are no seatbelts on your bike!"

Sure, it was a shot in the dark. I knew that often, when a motorcycle gets in a wreck, the last place you want to be is strapped onto it. In fact, motorcycle riders often survive wrecks by being thrown clear of the bike. But I also knew that the suit might just be enough to prompt a settlement. Sure enough, within days of filing, I got a call from the manufacturer's lead attorney.

"Gage," he said, "what the hell is wrong with you? Seatbelts? Really?"

"Scoff if you want," I said, "but my client would not have been launched over his handlebars had he been wearing a seatbelt. The public needs to know about this, don't you think? Heck, it could revolutionize the industry! I'm seeing seatbelts on every motorcycle!"

The company settled. Quickly. And my client was able to pay his medical bills. Unlike the bilingual warnings, however, I didn't suddenly start noticing seatbelts on motorcycles. If word got out about that particular brainchild of mine, it must have died pretty quickly. Rightfully so, I have to admit. It might make motorcycles less safe, not more. But the worst effect of such a law might just be this: scenes of Hells Angels straddling their hogs, roaring down desert highways, all wearing leather jackets and boots. And all buckled in for safety's sake.

CHAPTER SEVENTEEN

"We're Going to Get You"

OF ALL MY CASES in those Texas years, the biggest one was related to a credit collections agency, an agency whose business practices gave new meaning to the phrase "playing hardball."

The facts were roughly these: Marianne and Albert were a hardworking couple down on their luck. Marianne had lost her job and the two decided to pull up stakes, moving to El Paso from Massachusetts. Marianne found a job at an employee leasing company but Albert remained unemployed and money remained tight. Marianne called her creditors and pleaded for more time to pay and more favorable terms. She was determined to make good on her bills; she just needed some help and understanding. All her creditors were sympathetic and they all restructured her loans, accepting payments of ten dollars here and twenty dollars there whenever Marianne and Albert could afford to make them. All the creditors, that is, but one.

Marianne's Visa card was being serviced by a company called Household Credit. The balance was about $2,700 and they would hear nothing of restructuring it. And when Marianne began to get seriously behind on her payments, Household began to harass her, calling her at work and at home, sometimes four or five calls a day, sometimes early in the morning, sometimes late at night. And the calls weren't pretty.

"We're trying," Marianne pleaded on one phone call. "But my husband is out of work. I'll pay whatever I can."

"Listen," a Household representative said, according to Marianne's eventual testimony, "we don't want to hear any sob stories, *bitch*. We've heard it all. Just pay your goddamn bill!"

This went on for weeks, with Albert eventually taking the calls because of the toll the calls were taking on Marianne. Household ultimately turned the account over to Allied Adjustment Bureau, a collections agency. And then things got even worse.

One of Allied's collectors, who went by the name of Carol, called Marianne incessantly. "You better fucking pay," she'd say, "or we'll make your life here in El Paso miserable." One time she suggested that Marianne use a little imagination to find ways to come up with the money she owed. "Strap a mattress to your back, honey, and hit the streets." And then Carol started calling Marianne at work. Repeatedly. At times, the calls were so numerous that all of the company phone lines would be tied up. During one two-hour time period, Carol placed twenty-six calls to Marianne's work number.

Then one day someone else called Marianne. A guy by the name of Rick, who claimed to be Carol's supervisor, spoke calmly and evenly into the phone. "I just want you to know," he said, "that I've put a contract out on you. You better be careful entering and leaving your house because *we're going to get you*." Needless to say, Marianne was terrified.

The very next day there was a phone call at Marianne's work. Though the caller didn't identify herself, the receptionist recognized the voice. It was Carol. And Carol said, "You'd better evacuate. There's a bomb." The receptionist immediately called the police and Marianne's boss Gary called the FBI. No bomb was found but shortly thereafter, Marianne resigned, feeling she could no longer work effectively and no longer wished to expose the good people at the employee leasing firm to her personal problems. Gary, not exactly thrilled to have collection agencies tying up his company's phone lines with bomb threats, accepted her resignation.

By then, Marianne was so frightened of Allied and Household that she wasn't even able to leave her house. She and Albert made the decision to move and soon packed up and left for Truth or Consequences, New Mexico. At this point, Marianne began looking for legal help. The problem was that every lawyer she contacted said more or less the same thing: the case wouldn't be worth their time. All the lawyers, that is but one.

Ivy was always a soft touch. Sympathy and sentimentality often paved the way for decisions that ought to have been made on objective legal and business grounds. "I have a case you're going to try with me," she told me one morning. And then she said she'd taken a call from Marianne and began to describe the facts outlined above. I said something similar to what the other lawyers had said.

"How could you take this case?" I asked. "I mean, I feel for the poor woman, but she has no money. She's in debt, in fact. Obviously. And what are the grounds? What are the damages? Emotional distress? Do you know how hard that is to show?"

"I know, I know," said Ivy. "But I just felt sorry for her."

I groaned and shook my head. We had our work cut out for us.

I lined up a psychologist and deposed the relevant witnesses and did my research and prepared for trial. But of course I approached Household's lawyer first, a guy named Richard whom I happened to know, with the idea of a settlement.

"Richard," I offered, "let me have $150,000 to take care of this poor woman and let's settle this thing."

Richard talked it over with his client.

"He'll give you $15,000."

"Richard, I already spent more than that just to get my witnesses lined up." Richard said he was sorry but that was all he was authorized to offer. We had no choice but to take the case to trial.

My ace in the hole was the psychologist I'd found to interview Marianne. As the trial got underway, I called him to the stand and he testified very credibly in front of the jury that Marianne had suffered tremendously from the harassment from Household and their collections agency, Allied. I was pleased.

Then came Richard's cross-examination.

"Dr. Smith, would you mind telling the jury where you went to school?"

"The University of New Mexico," the doctor answered.

"And you have a PhD from there?"

"I earned a PhD from there, yes."

"Yes, but do you *have* a PhD from there, Doctor?"

"Well, no. Not any longer, that is."

"And would you mind telling the jury why you no longer have your PhD from the University of New Mexico?"

"Well, uh, they took it back. There was this charge of plagiarism and —."

"Thank you, Doctor. I have no further questions, Your Honor."

I wanted to crawl under the table. The doctor's confession was a stunner that I had not seen coming. Richard had done his homework—obviously better than I had done mine. I was losing credibility and I needed to think fast. I knew I needed to distance myself and my client from the doctor.

"Your Honor!" I jumped to my feet. "I am shocked and appalled at the admission of this doctor and I would like to request, for the sake of fairness to the defense, that his testimony, as helpful as it might have been to my client's case, be stricken from the record and that the jury be advised to disregard it." The maneuver stunned everyone in the courtroom. Who abandons valuable testimony? But I knew that telling a jury to disregard evidence they've heard is a bit like unringing a bell. My gambit was successful at keeping intact the integrity of our case while at the same time allowing the testimony of emotional distress to remain in the minds of the jurors, if not the written record.

The defense, as it turned out, had a psychologist of their own. Naturally he came to a different conclusion than ours: the source of Marianne's stress was not from Household or Allied, it was from her husband Albert. Albert was a heavy drinker who was, in addition to being unemployed, emotionally abusive, so said the psychologist. Now it was my turn to put a dent in their witness's testimony. As it happens, the psychologist was from Michigan and I knew all about him.

"Dr. Jones," I asked, "you're a forensic psychologist, is that correct?"

"Yes."

"And for the benefit of the jury, would you mind telling us what a forensic psychologist does?"

"Certainly. A forensic psychologist works with the court system on issues regarding the mental state of those involved in legal cases."

"And does a forensic psychologist get paid for that?"

"Of course."

"So in other words, you testify on behalf of companies like Household for money."

"Well, forensic psychologists perform a lot of different

services."

"I see. And what is your service here today?"

"To testify."

"On behalf of the defense?"

"Well, yes."

"For money?"

"Yes, of course. But look, I'm a trained psychologist." And then he added, "With a practice."

"And just how many patients do you currently have at this practice?"

"Well, at this particular time, I have ... well, I have one patient."

"One?"

"Yes, one."

"So is it safe to say that the bulk of your income comes from testifying in cases like these for defendants like Household?" Of course the doctor had no choice but to admit that his career was what I knew it to be in Michigan. He was a professional witness, bought and paid for by whoever needed expert psychological testimony. But the doctor held to his guns, insisting that he had, armed with a court order, interviewed both Albert and Marianne and had performed psychological tests that left him no doubt that Marianne's distress was caused more by her husband than by the debt collectors. I decided to take a different tack.

"And what are these tests, Doctor?" I asked.

"Well, one of them was a Rorschach test."

"I see. And isn't that the one where a patient observes an ink blot and says what he or she thinks it looks like?"

"That's essentially correct."

I walked up to the chalkboard and took a piece of chalk and turned it sideways, sweeping it back and forth over a portion of the board, producing a white shape.

"Would this be similar to your Rorschach test, Doctor?"

"Of course not," he grunted. "The Rorschach is an ink blot."

"I see." Then I took a bottle of ink from the court reporter's desk, spilled a little onto the center of a piece of paper, folded it over, and then opened it back up.

"How about this?" I said.

"Well, that would be more or less similar to the test," he admitted.

"Well, Doctor, I'm going to confess to you that, to me, this looks like ... hmmm ... I'd say a tree with birds in it."

"Okay."

"Now my question is this. If I think this shape looks like a tree with birds, and I show it to my wife Ivy, sitting there at the plaintiff's table, and she says it looks like berries in a field, which one of us would you say is crazy?" The courtroom laughed while the doctor tried to make some elaborate explanation as to the real use of the Rorschach test, but I knew it sounded like a bunch of medical jargon and I could sense the jury was becoming dubious.

In the meantime, the stress of the trial was becoming too much for Albert and Marianne. I had intended to call Albert to the stand but while waiting outside the courtroom, he began experiencing chest pains, actually going into mild cardiac arrest. An ambulance was called and as he was being loaded aboard, I heard Marianne say to him, "Albert, listen. This is too much for us. It's not worth it. I'm going to drop the case."

"No," Albert managed to say. "You go back in there and finish what you started. We can't let these bastards get away with what they've done. Don't worry about me." It inspired Marianne to continue, but it inspired me as well.

I called to the stand Gary, Marianne's boss at the

employee leasing firm. He wanted nothing to do with the case and came to the trial only by subpoena. But although he resented having to make an appearance, he testified about the bomb threat and the multitude of phone calls.

And I had one more trick up my sleeve. Before the trial, I had deposed one of the principals of Household Credit in his office in California. By then, Allied was essentially out of the picture. In time, they would actually declare bankruptcy (I imagine them, in a moment of perfect karma, getting harassed by debt collectors) but we were after Household under the legal principle of *respondeat superior*. Allied worked for Household and Household was, therefore, responsible for their actions. In any event, while deposing the principal of Household in his office, I noticed a child's framed water-color painting behind the man's desk. I casually asked him about it, a short conversation ostensibly about his seven-year-old son, the creator of the painting. But the conversation was on the record.

"Can you tell me," I said to him during the trial when he took the stand, "what's on the wall behind your desk in your office?"

"You mean the painting? It's a painting by my son."

"Do you have a good relationship with your son, sir?"

"Sure."

"Would you say he knows you well?"

"Yeah, sure. I mean, I'm his father."

"And could you tell the jury what the watercolor painting depicts?"

"It's a shark."

"Thank you, sir. I have no further questions."

The word "shark" stuck with the jury. I can't say it was necessarily the one and only thing that turned the trial in our favor, but it was at least the icing on the cake. After the trial, one of the jurors would say to me that the (stricken) testimony of our psychologist was far and above superior to the testimony of their psychologist (I wanted to ask, "But didn't you disregard it?" but thought better of it). I'd had Marianne testify, too, and she performed admirably. The jury could tell how stressful the entire affair had been for her. At any rate, however they got there, the jury returned a verdict in our favor. And did they ever. They awarded Marianne and Albert compensatory damages of two million dollars. And then, the next day, during the punitive phase of the case, they added nine million more to it.

Household owed Albert and Marianne eleven million dollars.

In the end, the case was appealed all the way to the Texas Supreme Court where the award was reduced to three million. Still, not a bad day's pay. As for Albert, who recovered from his heart attack, and Marianne, they took the money and bought a mobile home park in New Mexico where I like to think they lived happily ever after. As for me, the case made national news and was featured on the front page of *USA Today*. Bill Gates was on the front page, too. A story about his huge new product: Microsoft Windows 95. The difference? I was above the fold. Bill was below it.

CHAPTER EIGHTEEN
A Dish Best Served Cold

WHILE IN TEXAS, I took another interesting case, one I might never have decided to take except for an incident that had occurred years earlier in Detroit. I was still young at the time but already successful and with a reputation as an unbeatable trial attorney. And so it was that I received a phone call one day from a law firm in New York City, one of the largest firms in the world as a matter of fact. They were in need of an attorney to represent their Detroit client.

"We'd like to meet with you," said the voice on the phone, a partner with the New York law firm, a firm that shall be referred to herein as "Smith & Jones."

"Great," I said. "You're certainly welcome to come to Detroit and meet with me anytime."

"Well, we'd like you to come here," the partner said.

Though I was still young, I was beyond the days where I felt the necessity of having to fly somewhere to be interviewed for a job, no matter what firm was calling me. I was a successful attorney. If they wanted me, they knew where to find me.

"I'm sorry," I said, "I'm afraid that's impossible. My schedule just won't allow me to take the time to come to New York."

"I understand, Mr. Gage. But the thing is, there are four partners who are making the decision on what attorney to hire for this case and it would be a lot easier, I'm sure you'll agree, to fly one person rather than four. We're certainly willing to pay your expenses. First-class airfare, first-class accommodations. I'm certain you'll find it worth your while."

Well, okay, I thought, since he put it like that. Hell, if nothing else, it was a free trip to New York. I agreed and the arrangements were made. Two days later I flew into JFK. When I arrived, one of the partners—the firm's only female partner—was waiting for me in the firm's limo. It was winter and it was cold and I had worn a heavy, rather bright tan overcoat.

"It's a pleasure to meet you, Mr. Gage," she said. "I'm Anne." And then I noticed Anne eyeing my coat. "We'll be going to the office to meet the other partners involved with this case shortly. First, though, if you don't mind, I'd like to make a quick stop at Paul Stuart's on Madison Avenue. We'll need to replace that overcoat of yours, I'm afraid."

"Excuse me? My overcoat? This is vicuña."

"Yes, of course, but you see, Mr. Gage, it was my idea to bring you here. I'm the one who researched and found you. And I really need for this to go well. Your coat is … well, it's fine, but we don't want to leave anything to chance. We need you to look your absolute best and I'm afraid that color … well, it doesn't really work, does it? You understand, I'm sure. Oh, don't worry about the cost. It'll be my expense."

With that, the limo headed for Paul Stuart's, where I was sent inside for a new overcoat, which, of course, required the proper hat and gloves to match. The bill was well over a thousand dollars but Anne seemed pleased. My vicuña coat, meanwhile, was boxed up courtesy of the store and shipped back to my office in Detroit.

"Much better," Anne said. "Thank you for humoring me. You understand, I'm sure." That was the second time she'd said that. I really didn't understand, as a matter of fact, but I said nothing.

At the office of Smith & Jones, I sat across from Anne and three of the other partners as they asked me some basic questions about my background and then they inquired about my hourly fee.

"That's a little high for a Michigan attorney," they said after I had told them what I charged.

"Well, what can I say? I'm a high-priced lawyer," I smiled, wanting to add, *in a high-priced coat and hat.* "Listen," I said. "Why don't you tell me about the case?"

The partners laid out the basic facts. Two siblings were in dispute over a probate matter of roughly $300 million in G.M. stock. Their client was in Michigan. His brother was in New York laying claim to half the stock. But the New York brother was an adopted family member, an adoption that occurred after his eighteenth birthday, thus throwing into doubt his legal rights to the stock. It seemed like a very winnable case.

"Tell you what," I said. "Since my fee seems to be an issue, let's cut it in half. And I'll take five percent of any recovery." The partners agreed, murmuring to each other about how they probably should have structured their own compensation that way with the client.

I flew back to Detroit and began putting the case together. When the first probate hearing was scheduled, I called New York to notify Smith & Jones as a matter of professional courtesy, to keep them in the loop. It was a routine procedural hearing and I assured them it would go well. But when I entered the courtroom for the hearing, I saw, to my utter surprise, three of the Smith & Jones partners sitting in the front row. *They weren't willing to come to Detroit to interview me but are suddenly willing to fly out to watch me in a routine procedural hearing?* I put the distraction out of my mind and addressed the judge, presenting the guts of my case. He asked some questions, which I answered. Then came the second surprise of the day.

"I find Mr. Gage's argument to be very persuasive," the judge said. "I don't see any reason to try this case. I'll have my written opinion rendered within two weeks."

I'd won. Without so much as a trial.

In the hallway, the partners shook my hand and congratulated me. I went back to the office ecstatic. Now, as it happens, this was shortly after I had merged my firm with Herzfeld and Rubin in New York for the product liability cases we were arguing on behalf of the automobile manufacturer. Naturally, Herzfeld and Rubin would get a piece of the recovery and I imagined how thrilled they'd be with their new partner in Detroit. I had done the math. Five percent of $300 million was $15 million. My life would never be the same.

Three days later, a letter arrived from Smith & Jones. "Thank you for your service," the letter read. "Please accept this as official notification that we will be discharging you from your responsibilities on the case you had represented on our behalf. Due to an ethical conflict, we have no choice but to sever our relationship with your firm. Again, we thank you."

I picked myself up off the floor and placed a phone call to Smith & Jones. Anne took the call.

"I'm sorry, Noel," she said. "The other side of the case has consulted with an attorney at Herzfeld and Rubin. Naturally that presents a conflict of interest, since your firm is affiliated with them." Later I learned what had really happened. The adversary in the case had a brief lunch with Herb Rubin at which point Herb promptly turned the case down, probably because he knew the adversary's case wasn't any good. That was the extent of the so-called consultation.

"Look," I said to Anne, "this is an easy enough fix. We'll just build a Chinese wall." It was a legal expression describing an information barrier erected between parts of an organization, like a law firm, that might have competing interests. It was a perfectly legitimate tool and ours seemed simple enough to set up. Herb and I were in different cities, after all.

"We can't take the chance, Noel," said Anne. "But I can't tell you how much we've appreciated your help. I'll see to it that the check for your full hourly fee is sent right out."

And then she hung up. She hung up before I had the chance to tell her where to stick the check. And the overpriced Paul Stuart coat, for that matter. It was obvious what was happening. There was no conflict of interest. Somehow word had gotten back to Smith & Jones that Herb had had lunch with the other party to the case and it was all they needed to hear to get rid of me and my claim to fifteen million dollars. The fifteen million would remain with Smith & Jones. The client had already agreed to it. Meanwhile, Anne had said "full" hourly fee as though she was doing me a huge favor. Eventually I would force myself to stop thinking about what I would have done with the money or what the partners at Smith & Jones did with it. Did they all buy new homes? Send all their children through Harvard? It was wrong, what they did, but it was perfectly legal. I'd been screwed.

Fifteen years went by. By then, I'd moved to El Paso. While there, I settled a case against a pharmaceutical company based in California. During the negotiations I guess I must have impressed the company's general counsel. His best friend was in need of an attorney with my level of expertise and he recommended me.

"Josh has told me great things about you," Andy said, when he called me one morning from California.

171

"Well, I hope I can help," I said. "Tell me about your case."

Andy described his situation. He was a very light-skinned African-American, his mother being Caucasian but his father being of Ethiopian descent. So light-skinned was Andy that nobody he worked with knew he was actually an African-American, as he would come to learn. He was an attorney, working in the Los Angeles office of a prestigious New York City law firm and working hard. Andy was young and aggressive, taking on a workload of close to 3,000 billable hours per year, doing millions of dollars of work for the firm and impressing everyone in the office.

But just after the L.A. riots in 1992, Andy's law firm took on a high-ranking police official as a client. On a particular Sunday, Andy went into the office to get some work done and walked past a conference room where a couple of the partners were meeting with the police official. What he heard was stunning. Words like "spearchuckers" and "jigaboos" and "niggers" were being casually tossed about to describe the participants in the riots. Andy was absolutely aghast.

That Monday, he went into the managing partner's office and reported what he'd heard the day before. "Yeah, that's kind of rude," said the managing partner. "I'll have to talk to those guys about it."

"No," said Andy, "you don't understand. I'm here to file a formal complaint. That was inexcusable behavior for the workplace."

"But, Andy," said the partner, "I mean, sure, those guys shouldn't be using language like that, but what do you care?"

Andy paused. "You don't know?"

"No."

"I care because I'm an African-American."

The managing partner was shocked. He'd had no idea.

He hemmed and hawed and then eventually agreed to address the matter with the head office in New York. A couple days later, one of the New York partners called Andy and apologized and said they would take a very active stance on the matter and make sure nothing like that would ever happen again. It was lip service. Nothing was ever done.

But then things got worse. Suddenly Andy found himself with his workload cut back. From an annualized count of 3,000 hours, he was down to 500. The firm was giving cases to seemingly everyone but Andy. He overheard comments being made, too, about blacks in general and about himself in particular. "Andy's so stupid because he's half black," he heard a senior associate say. "Bet he got his law degree through affirmative action," someone else remarked. The discrimination was so sickening to him that he felt he had no choice but to resign. And then he started calling law firms to represent him in a discrimination case. I wasn't the first.

"Everybody else has turned me down," he told me on the phone that morning.

"Well, Andy," I said, "I sympathize, but you can see why. Discrimination cases are really hard to prove. It's he-said, she-said. And I'm sure the firm has extremely deep pockets. It's the kind of case that can really drag out. At best, it's an uphill climb. I'm sorry. I wish you well but I'm afraid I'm going to have to turn the case down as well."

"I understand," said Andy. "Well, thanks for listening. I'll keep looking. There's just no way I'm going to let those bastards at Smith & Jones get away with what they did."

"Well, good luck, maybe — wait, *what* did you say?"

"I said I'm going to keep looking for an attorney."

"No, the law firm. The firm you worked for. What firm did you say it was?"

"Smith & Jones. Why?"

"Andy, how soon can you fly here to see me? We've got a lot of work to do and the quicker we get started the better."

I'd waited fifteen years for Andy's phone call. Truthfully, I would have taken the case for free. I explained to him my reasons, feeling it was only right to do so.

"It's okay with me," he said. "Whatever your reasons are, I'm just grateful you're taking the case."

I wasn't licensed to practice in California but I was able to find a lawyer to sponsor me, and Andy and I sued Smith & Jones in California Superior Court. The New York office of Smith & Jones hired a California firm to represent them. The person in charge of the hiring? The same person that hired me fifteen years prior: Anne.

During the depositions, I beat their guys up pretty bad. I asked one of their partners, "Have you ever used the term nigger?"

"Not recently," he said without thinking. "I mean ... no!"

"No or 'not recently'?" I asked.

All the depositions went more or less like that. Smith & Jones was in a deep hole and I was having a blast.

For Andy's part, he was flawless. With a photographic memory, Andy turned out to be the smartest lawyer I had ever encountered. After three days of deposing him at Century Plaza Hotel in Los Angeles, one of the lawyers representing Smith & Jones asked him a question Andy was sure had already been asked.

"I don't think so," said the lawyer when Andy told him he'd provided his answer two days before.

"Check the record," said Andy, who, the preceding night, had read the transcripts from the previous two days. "Look on page 546, line 21." That ended Andy's deposition. The Smith & Jones side was quickly learning that they were out-matched.

Then things got even better for us as the trial got underway. Court TV had decided to air it. I was going to be able to humiliate Smith & Jones on national television. And when the jury was impaneled, we managed to make sure half of it was composed of African-Americans. Smith & Jones was going down.

And that's when I got a phone call from Anne. "We want to settle," she said.

"I'm sure you do," I replied. "Make an offer if you'd like. I'm ethically obligated to pass it along to my client. But you should know that I also plan to advise him to tell you to stick your offer, whatever it is, where the sun don't shine."

Anne made a low offer, which was unsurprising, of half a million dollars. I took it back to Andy, fully expecting he'd reject it and we'd continue to trial. But Andy had other ideas.

"Look, Noel," he said. "My circumstances have changed. I've been offered an opportunity to teach at Harvard and I'm going to take it. I don't want to practice anymore. I want to get on with my life. Take their offer to settle."

I was crushed. I'd smelled blood. Revenge—fifteen years in the making—was in reach. We could have gotten millions. I argued with Andy against taking Smith & Jones's first offer, but to no avail. He was the client and he knew what he wanted and I had to go along with it. In the end, I knew it was about him, not me.

"But Noel," he said, "I'm going to insist they reimburse me for my legal fees. Send me a bill. And double it."

Fifteen years earlier, Smith & Jones had paid me my hourly fee and no more. Andy at least was now making sure they'd be paying twice the fee. It was small consolation, but it was something. Plus, the case had cost them at least a half million dollars. And it went down in history as the first race discrimination lawsuit by an attorney to result in a significant settlement against a major firm.

I wasn't going to ever be able to beat Smith & Jones to the tune I had wanted. But I'd done right by my client and I had performed my duties legally *and* ethically, something I knew Anne and the others at Smith & Jones couldn't quite say about their own way of doing things. It wasn't much. It certainly wasn't fifteen million dollars. But it was enough.

CHAPTER NINETEEN

Viva Las Vegas

EVENTUALLY, IVY AND I would leave Texas. We wanted a better, more challenging school for our daughter. She was a bright kid and we determined she could benefit by a better education than what was then available in the El Paso area. I had three conditions for moving. First, of course, wherever we moved needed to have the schooling we were looking for. Second, it needed to have warm weather like Texas. I wasn't about to go back to the days of Michigan winters. Third, also like Texas, it needed to be a place free of state income tax.

Steve Parsons was a fellow member of the American Bar Association. At one time, I'd been the Michigan appointee to the Forum Committee on Franchising and Steve had been a Bar Association delegate from Nevada. Steve was a great guy and we'd become friends. Talking with him one time on the phone from Texas, I mentioned my desire to move and shared with him my conditions.

The Forum on Franchising, incidentally, had been a great experience for me. I'd been appointed by the president of the Michigan Bar at the time—Wallace Riley—and while on the committee, I persuaded Ambassador John Gavin, a client of mine, to give the keynote dinner speech. John was appointed by President Reagan as U.S. Ambassador to Mexico, but of course he was more than just that. John was an accomplished actor with roles in some famous movies, like *Spartacus* and *Psycho*. There was a time, in fact, when he'd been signed on to play the role of James Bond in *Diamonds Are Forever*, before Sean Connery was cajoled into coming back to do one more Bond film. In his later career John would turn up from time to time on popular television shows like *Fantasy Island* and *The Love Boat*. His wife Constance was an accomplished actress in her own right and I had the pleasure of watching her, from a front row seat, perform opposite Yul Brynner in *The King and I*. Anyway, John Gavin's dinner speech was a big hit and members of the committee told me it was the best dinner the group had ever had.

In any event, I talked to Steve Parsons about what I was looking for in a new home and he said, "Then come to Las Vegas. We've got everything you're looking for right here. Come visit and I'll give you a tour." Of course all I'd ever seen of Vegas was the airport and the Strip but I agreed to come out and let Steve show us around. We were impressed. There were beautiful residential areas and the whole town, outside of the Strip, seemed like a great place to live. So, after a relatively short deliberation, we decided to move to Vegas where Ivy and I opened Gage and Gage Law Firm.

I met some interesting people in Vegas, one of whom was a neighbor across the street from my home. Yohan Lowie was a builder and a genius. He had very little formal training in architecture but nevertheless went on to design and build amazing properties around the Las Vegas area including a couple projects that together, I consider to be the eighth wonders of the world—One Queensridge Place and Tivoli Village. Queensridge is two eighteen-story residential towers that boast some of the most exclusive, expensive custom homes in the country. The penthouses at the top are 15,000 square feet each. Tivoli Village is thirty-five acres of retail space built like an old-world village, complete with a town square and bell tower. Stones from thirty different countries were used, as well as the services of a thousand artists, to create beautiful floors and ceilings and walls, a veritable mosaic of stonework.

Not bad for a guy who started his career in security. Working out of California, Yohan was in charge of the personal security detail for Meshulam Riklis, a successful businessman from Israel. Riklis had a string of profitable ventures, but might best be known today as the guy who tried, unsuccessfully, to make Pia Zadora a star. At the age of fifty-three, Riklis divorced his wife and married Zadora, thirty years his junior. Then he financed a film with her as the lead actress. Unfortunately, the film was heavily panned by the critics and a box office flop as well.

But at one time, Riklis owned the famed Riviera Hotel and Casino in Vegas and one day Yohan, whom Riklis had taken a liking to, told his boss that he'd like to try his hand at building high end homes around Las Vegas. Riklis offered to finance Yohan, but Yohan wanted to make it on his own, partially financing his first project with a revolving credit card from Sears. The rest, as they say, is history and today, with One Queensridge Place and Tivoli Village to his credit, Yohan is still very active in real estate development.

Yohan was a Gage and Gage client for a while, but eventually, I knew he needed more expertise than I could offer him in the area of real estate transactional law. I referred him to Alan Sklar, one of the best in the country in that field. Alan and Yohan have both become dear friends of mine; as has Bret Harrison, whom I introduced to Yohan and who works for him now. Bret was a Navy SEAL, top in his class. It was fascinating getting to know all these guys.

Another interesting person I would eventually get to know in Las Vegas was Ivan Goldsmith, a doctor who runs a highly successful weight-loss clinic. He's also skilled in family medicine, internal medicine, and geriatrics. His crusade these days is in stopping legislation that seeks to make it ever more difficult for doctors to prescribe pain relief medication to their patients. Ivan is a proponent of the use of medical marijuana and a real voice for those who, through chronic illness or injury, have a genuine need for pain management.

As for Gage and Gage, we did well upon our arrival to the Las Vegas legal scene. I continued taking on medical malpractice suits, among other cases, and adjusted quickly to my new surroundings. One thing I didn't have at the outset, however, was a good local M.D. who could testify for me as an expert witness in those malpractice suits. Finding doctors willing to testify against other doctors is problematic to begin with. Very few want to risk it. They become pariahs, ostracized by their colleagues. Add to that the fact that you can't rely on just any doctor to testify. You need a highly credentialed one, someone who has knowledge and experience and can speak eloquently and won't fold under the pressure of cross-examination.

With this in mind, I began sitting in on medical malpractice trials, scouting for an expert witness I could make use of: looking for someone who could impress a jury. I found one in short order. I watched as one doctor in particular delivered his testimony during a certain trial, and his delivery was sure and convincing. I approached him after the day's proceedings, introducing myself as a relatively new attorney in town seeking help for the clients of mine who'd been victimized by medical negligence and malpractice.

"Well, I don't really talk to lawyers," he said to my surprise.

"Well, how did you come to testify in court today?" I asked.

"I was brought in by a medical consultant. Howard Awand. He works with aggrieved patients, finding attorneys for them and connecting them with expert witnesses."

Howard Awand sounded like a guy I needed to know.

"Can you give him my card?" I said.

"Sure."

A few days later, Howard called and we met. I was immediately impressed. Howard had gone to med school but never graduated, having elected to serve instead as an Army medic, winning commendations along the way. His knowledge of medicine was comprehensive and over time he'd made himself a nice consulting business by helping victims of malpractice successfully sue doctors. This, it must be understood, is no easy feat. Doctors don't pay judgments; their insurers do. And the insurance industry has extraordinarily deep pockets. The deck is always stacked against the plaintiff. Of course I knew from my own experience how hard it can be, but I'd made a good living from it and after Howard learned of my successes in Michigan and Texas, he became as impressed with me as I was with him. The meeting was very productive for both of us.

Soon, Howard began referring a few of his consulting clients to me. Then he'd remain involved, lining up expert witnesses for the cases, doing research, even preparing the cross-examination of the defendant's experts. The collaboration was effective and the results were outstanding. It was known that, generally speaking, doctors and their insurance companies won ninety percent of malpractice cases. We represented the ten percent that they'd lose, the ten percent in which the doctors were called to account for harm caused by shoddy technique or just plain negligence. We were a voice for the lone patient (or his or her family) against the enormous resources of the huge insurance companies. It was gratifying.

In one case, a forty-two-year-old man went into the

hospital for surgery to have a kidney stone removed. The surgery was supposed to be routine. But the surgeon nicked an artery, unaware that he'd done so. Worse, he didn't bother to check on the man in recovery. The man bled internally and by the time it was noticed by the hospital staff, the patient had become brain-dead. The insurance company, meanwhile, knew that the man's death would be a lot cheaper than keeping him alive on life-support. This is the way insurance companies work. It's profit and loss. It's income and expense. It's bottom line. And that may explain why the man was moved from the critical care unit of intensive care to a step-down unit, even though he was on a respirator and had a raging fever. It might also explain why he was situated directly in front of a cold air-conditioning vent.

Now, I couldn't prove any intent to kill on the part of the insurance company, but they knew what a jury might do if the implication was clearly made. And that's why they settled. For $18 million. You don't settle for such a sum if you think you're going to win. It was a well-deserved number, as far as I was concerned, and it was also one of the biggest settlements of my career. But little did I know what it would lead to. The case reverberated throughout the insurance industry and my name became well known. And not in a good way. I was their enemy and I was now in their crosshairs. And it turns out that the insurance industry has some pretty powerful friends. More powerful than I could have ever imagined. How far would they go to protect their own?

It wouldn't take long for me to find out. One evening I was watching the local news on television and a story aired about three law firms "currently under investigation by the FBI." Naturally, I perked up. Which of my esteemed colleagues was in trouble? I recognized the names of the first two firms—big law firms, much bigger than ours. And I wondered what could possibly be the nature of the investigation. But then they named the third: "Gage and Gage." My jaw dropped open. It was a hell of way to learn that my law practice was being investigated by the feds.

CHAPTER TWENTY
Sometimes Goliath Wins

Wherever law ends, Tyranny begins
– John Locke

IF THE INSURANCE industry's pockets are deep, the federal government's are positively bottomless, with every means at their disposal for winning any case they decide to prosecute. Often, the decisions about whom to go after are made politically. They'll start with an investigation to find something and keep looking even if there's nothing there. Then comes the indictment. Now, there's an old saying that you can indict a ham sandwich. Indictments mean nothing. But once indicted, win or lose, your reputation is forever besmirched. And from there, federal prosecutors, with little to no oversight, can make up the rules as they go.

I could never prove that the insurance industry was behind the FBI investigation and my eventual indictment, but the coincidence was too much to reasonably dismiss. I negotiate an $18 million settlement and suddenly the feds are after me? I hadn't done anything except beat the insurer fair and square. The federal charge? Something called honest services fraud. It's a catch-all term and a tool that the feds can use to move against somebody when they really don't have anything else. Essentially, it refers to "a scheme or artifice to deprive another of the intangible right of honest services." It's mainly used against public figures, and the feds like to throw around terms like bribes and kickbacks; but the statute is not without its critics. U.S. Supreme Court Justice Antonin Scalia has said it's so poorly defined that it could be the basis for prosecuting "a mayor for using the prestige of his office to get a table at a restaurant without a reservation."

In fact, my attorney, at considerable expense to me, prepared a comprehensive white paper for the head prosecutor during his investigation prior to the indictment, outlining in thorough detail, using case study as well as my specific circumstances, the obvious lack of legal grounds for pursuing a case against me. The prosecutor was unmoved. To the amazement of my attorney, the prosecutor told him (off the record, naturally), "I don't care. We're going to just let a bunch of shit fly and see what sticks."

I was arrested on my sixty-ninth birthday and the federal case against me was roughly this: I had "conspired" with Howard Awand and two surgeons to shift the blame for an allegedly botched surgery from those surgeons to the anesthesiologist. Here were the facts: a woman had back surgery. The surgeon then went on a planned vacation, leaving the woman in the care of his associate, another surgeon. Shortly thereafter, minor, but not entirely unpredictable complications arose. Some fluid needed to be drained from the spine with the use of a catheter. This required an anesthesiologist and the anesthesiologist made several clumsy mistakes in the placement of the spinal catheter. Perhaps I should say "placements," as it turned out the anesthesiologist inserted the catheter twelve separate times before deciding to leave the patient be. His efforts resulted in the woman becoming tragically paralyzed.

The case was referred to me by Howard, and Howard arranged for me to meet with the two surgeons in question (the original one and his associate) who were able to convince me, through the kind of questioning that I usually reserved for cross-examinations in court, that the fault was not with them, but with the anesthesiologist. It turns out, however, that these two doctors often worked with Howard; he utilized them as expert witnesses. But I didn't know them and I felt no loyalty to them in any way. In fact, after my questioning, I did my own independent research to confirm their opinion about the anesthesiologist. And then my clients—the paralyzed woman and her husband—proceeded to file suit against the anesthesiologist. It was, in my mind, clearly the proper course of action and we ended up settling to the tune of two-plus million dollars.

But the government, seeking a way (any way) to nail me on an honest services fraud charge, claimed the meeting with the surgeons was somehow "secret" and conspiratorial. We had all "agreed" that I would sue the anesthesiologist and not the surgeons. I would be paid back with a lucrative referral from Howard. This constituted a "kickback." The government's "proof" was that I did indeed have more cases referred to me by Howard. But of course, that was the nature of our business relationship. Howard knew I could represent his clients better than anyone and so he referred them to me. And my loyalty was to the clients, not to Howard and not to any doctors he happened to work with. In truth, I had, some-time earlier, not hesitated to sue another doctor who also happened to be in Howard's circle, a personal friend of his, in fact.

Additional "evidence" was the government's opinion that I should have been able to secure more than two-million dollars for my clients. I didn't get enough, in their minds. I should have been able to get somewhere around ten million had I also included the surgeons in the suit (notwithstanding the fact that I found no negligence on their parts and seriously doubted a jury would, either). The fact is that the client had originally been offered $700,000 and by coming to me, her award had been tripled.

But no matter how weak the government's case (the honest services fraud charge would eventually be tossed out by the presiding judge, after which the relevant law itself would be neutered by the Supreme Court), that didn't stop them from trying

When the government makes up its mind to go after somebody, they use every trick in the book. And they have a bunch of them. One of those tricks is to "leak" information to the media. This is how the local television station learned of the investigation even before I did. The idea is to manufacture adverse publicity so as to render you guilty in the eyes of the public even before a trial. Even before an indictment. It's not hard to imagine what this does for an attorney's practice. Clients left. My source of income dried up. Fighting the government is expensive and the government's strategy is often one of war by attrition. Win or lose, they'll starve you out.

Other tricks include delaying the proceedings by any means possible, filing motion after motion—another way to force you to burn through your savings. I continually asserted my right to a speedy trial, but in the end, my fight against the government took years. And of course that's the way they want it. They also like to bury you in paperwork. Thousands upon thousands of exhibits and documents were threatened to be entered into evidence. Hundreds were entered, the vast majority of which held no relevance but nevertheless needed to be reviewed thoroughly for fear of missing something that could be used against me.

Naturally, they also continued to feed information to the media on a nearly daily basis. My name was constantly in the news. It seemed every day there was an article about my case. *Fortune* did a piece about Howard (also indicted), calling his group of physicians and attorneys the "medical mafia" and dragging my name into it. I was interviewed for the article and told them the truth. They quoted me accurately: "I don't believe there is a medical mafia, and if there is, I am certainly not aligned with it. [The government investigators] are despicable, dishonest human beings [who have not proved] one scintilla of criminality." But of course it doesn't matter what you say. Once your name gets put into such an article, you are forever in the mind of the public guilty of *something*. And after the fraud charge was thrown out, I sure don't remember seeing a follow-up article in *Fortune* describing how wrong the government was.

If all of this had adverse effects on my practice and my bank account, it was nothing compared to the effect on my family. The kids heard about it at school ("Your dad's a crook!") and we eventually had to send them to California to finish their schooling in relative peace. Meanwhile, Ivy and I began fighting over whether or not I should just plead guilty and get it over with. The government made several offers to me for a guilty plea. This is how most of their cases end. A guilty plea means victory for them. Taking the case to trial means a jury and a case like mine would have meant defeat. U.S. attorneys are appointed and feel an allegiance to those who appoint them, not necessarily to the truth. They're paid to win. And most use the position as a stepping stone to something higher, often looking to eventually become federal judges. Consequently, their win-loss record is all that really matters to them. And so they'll use the tricks at their disposal to eventually exhaust a defendant to the point where he'll plead guilty, typically to a lesser charge for a reduced sentence. That way, they secure their victory without the risk of trial.

Ivy understandably wanted the nightmare to end. "Just plead!" she'd say. I refused. "But I'm not guilty of anything!" I'd shoot back. "How can I plead guilty if I'm not guilty and still look at myself in the mirror?" Ultimately, the pressure was too much. We divorced. Not content to destroy my practice, the government destroyed my family as well.

In the end, after every effort the government could make, after the honest services fraud charge was thrown out, the only thing the government had was a flimsy charge of obstruction of justice. They had subpoenaed every check my firm had written to Howard. The checks were part of a monumental list of items they had subpoenaed. My office manager inadvertently failed to turn over one of the checks. But of course it was my law practice and the buck stops with me. I accepted that. Out of money, out of options, years into the legal fight, I tendered an Alford plea, an assertion of innocence but a concession that you won't, or can't, continue to defend yourself. The result was technically a "conviction" but my satisfaction, if there is any, is that an Alford plea doesn't statistically count as a victory for the prosecution.

Meanwhile, the government spent untold amounts of taxpayer money on the case. Tens of millions of dollars would be my guess. Frequently in court they'd had a dozen attorneys or more. Behind the scenes, there were dozens more. The FBI, the largest investigative agency in the world, was looking under every rock for whatever they could find. My sentence was 90 days home confinement and a $25,000 fine. Oh, and I had to pay back my fee to the client who had suffered the botched spinal procedure, the one for whom I had "only" secured two-million dollars.

Unfortunately, even with the Alford plea, the Nevada Bar considered it as a bona-fide conviction and my license to practice was suspended. I would eventually be able to reapply. But of course, my reputation was in tatters and my family had been torn apart. Such is the unchecked power of the federal government.

CHAPTER TWENTY-ONE

Epilogue

EVEN HAVING SPENT my entire career as a lawyer, having to deal with the federal prosecution system in the role of the accused was eye-opening for me. In retrospect, I suppose it should not have been. We like to think that in the United States, with our beautiful and ingenious Constitution, our rights as citizens are protected. That the government is looking out for us. That even if we are accused of a crime, our case will be handled fairly and ethically. We'll be presumed innocent unless the evidence says otherwise beyond a shadow of a doubt. But what we forget—what I forgot and learned the hard way—is that the government is operated by people. In all their flawed glory. Any legal system devised by humankind, no matter how perfect it might seem, is only as good as the humans who run it. People in our American justice system are no different than people in any other line of work; they're often motivated by all the wrong things: fear, ambition, greed, ego. And if these motivations are all that are propelling you, then the rule of law becomes something not to respect and work within, but rather to work around. You look for any advantage you can get, ethics be damned. You cut corners. You cheat.

Mine is but one example. The examples are everywhere. In March of 2006, a stripper was called to perform at a house party in Durham, North Carolina. The house was occupied by the lacrosse team of Duke University. There was apparent disagreement over the woman's performance and her compensation, and she left. Later that same night, she accused three members of the team of raping her. The three young men were soon arrested for first degree forcible rape, first degree sexual offense, and kidnapping. The media got hold of the story in no time, thanks in large part to the district attorney who just happened to be running for re-election in a very tight race. During one week alone, the D.A. gave, by his own estimate, between fifty and seventy interviews, spending more than forty hours with reporters.

The media are never blameless in these cases, either. News of the alleged rapes made front page headlines from coast to coast. Bowing to national pressure, the university shut down the lacrosse team for the remainder of the season and forced the head coach to resign. Naturally, the three accused players were ejected from the university. Guilt, in other words, was assumed. Judgment had been rendered—if not in court, then in the minds of the public. Reputations were ruined.

For the players' part, being kicked out of school was the least of their worries. They were facing years and years in prison, their lives essentially over. Of course there was only one problem with the district attorney's case. After all the evidence came in, it turned out he really didn't have one. The stripper kept changing her story, eyewitness accounts and DNA evidence exonerated the accused, and it was revealed that the Durham Police Department had taken a few shortcuts themselves in their handling of the case to the disfavor of the players. The charges were dismissed. The players were innocent.

These kinds of examples abound. The Duke case is one of the more famous ones, but for every Duke case, there are a dozen more. Every day, someone is falsely accused by a prosecutor, or team of prosecutors, and the prosecution, in its zeal and arrogance and unrestrained ambition, will unilaterally decide the accused is guilty, enlist the media to press the point, and proceed to destroy a life and a reputation. It's the shame of America.

Just how perverse is the prosecutorial system? How untouchable are prosecutors? No less than a Supreme Court justice has argued that a prosecutor "may receive absolute immunity from suit for acts violating the Constitution in order to advance important societal values." Justice Elena Kagan, an Obama appointee to the Court, asserted this mind-numbing idea while Solicitor-General. In that role, she argued before the Supreme Court in apparent support of fabricated evidence. In a brief to the Court, she quoted a lower court opinion: "We do not see how the existence of a false police report, sitting in a drawer in a police station, by itself deprives a person of a right secured by the Constitution and laws." It's anything goes for prosecutors, in other words, so long as the fabricated evidence isn't actually used in court. No harm, no foul. Of course there's no mention of how the case gets to court in the first place. No mention of how prosecutors use fabricated evidence to make witnesses talk or to bully people into confessions or guilty pleas. Presumably, all of that is acceptable so long as we're advancing "important societal values."

The opinion quoted by Kagan came from the case of Pottawattamie versus McGhee where it was essentially argued, on behalf of prosecutors for the Iowa county of Pottawattamic, that there is no constitutional right not to be framed. Curtis McGhee and Terry Harrington were two African-American kids in the summer of 1977 when a sixteen-year-old, arrested for car theft, fingered them for the shooting of a night security guard at a car dealership in Council Bluffs. It didn't seem to matter to police and prosecutors that the statements of the sixteen-year-old witness, who was desperate to have his car theft charges dropped, were contradictory and inaccurate on key details. It also didn't seem to matter that another suspect in the shooting, a white man, failed a lie detector test; that suspect was released after the statement from the young car thief, and the prosecutors went after McGhee and Harrington. An all-white jury convicted the two, based mostly on the witness testimony.

McGhee and Harrington spent twenty-six years in prison. Ultimately, they were able to obtain files that revealed the prosecutors compelled the sixteen-year-old to testify (he eventually recanted) and buried evidence that implicated the original white suspect. McGhee and Harrington's sentences were subsequently overturned, whereupon they sued the prosecutors. An Iowa court rendered the opinion that Kagan quoted, and McGhee and Harrington appealed, all the way to the Supreme Court. The Supreme Court justices heard arguments (including Kagan's) in 2009. There was reason to believe they would decide in favor of McGhee and Harrington, thus reversing the incredibly un-American principle that a prosecutor can actually frame a suspect without running afoul of the U.S. Constitution. That prosecutors can't be sued for fabricating evidence was called "a strange proposition" by Justice Kennedy and "perverse" by Justice Stevens. Alas, Pottawattamie County settled with McGhee and Harrington for twelve million dollars before any opinion was inked. It's a shame the case wasn't decided by the Supreme Court, but who can fault the two victims of prosecutorial power run amuck for taking the money? Hopefully another case will ultimately come along that will correct this scandalous flaw in our American system of justice. Perhaps the editorial of August 30, 2015 in the *New York Times* will spur such a case on.

A recent article by Bethany Barnes in the *Las Vegas Review Journal* (November 8, 2015) also put the spotlight on the injustices of the prosecutorial system. It's encouraging to see some of this finally coming to light.

⌐

Time, they say, heals all wounds. But there will never be enough time for me to forget what the federal government did to me. But I won't wallow, either. That's not exactly my style. Now, with my license to practice law finally reinstated (and, I might add, by a unanimous decision by the Nevada Supreme Court), I am ready to piece back together my reputation. It won't take long. I'm confident that my level of expertise will ultimately trump the damage inflicted by the government. My success will return clients to me and I can get on with my life's work.

As for the unwarranted interruption, I have been using the downtime to do a little traveling and to put together these memoirs. And to reconnect with my kids. That hasn't necessarily been easy. If I have one regret, it's that I did not spend enough time with my children while they were growing up. My career was one of sixteen-hour days, seven days a week. But it's the only way I knew how to operate: a work ethic cultivated long ago, pulling two shifts a day in the summers selling Good Humor ice cream. Clients depended on me. I think especially of the medical malpractice cases, up against the mega insurance companies, and I know an extraordinary effort was required to provide my clients with some restitution for the harm done to them by negligent doctors. It took nothing less than total commitment.

I have three grandkids now, too. One is a recent Harvard graduate, one is set for a career in architecture, and one is just entering college. Whole lifetimes ahead of them. I envy them in some ways, but would anybody really want to go back and relive those years? Once is more than enough. For me, it's hard to imagine having done anything else with my life, although sometimes I think I'd have made a hell of a physician. I know for a fact that I'd have had a better bedside manner than what's prevalent these days. And I'd have made house calls to boot.

But it seems I was destined to be a lawyer, ever since I watched as a lawyer helped my parents with their legal fight against the neighbors. Ever since my undergraduate days at Michigan and then law school. By the time I started working with Leonard, there was no going back. No second-guessing. Not even after my interview with the stripper who only stopped stabbing her boyfriend because the knife broke. Not even after losing my very first case because of the judge's golfing relationship with the opposing counsel. Not even after the man called wanting to sue the applesauce company after purposely eating applesauce he knew contained glass.

From those humble days, I was launched into a career that included the successful defense of frivolous lawsuits against a major automobile manufacturer, high-profile triumphs against major corporations and law firms that were engaged in racial discrimination, a huge victory over a menacing collections agency, and about a thousand other cases, each with its own distinctive set of interesting circumstances. Along the way I've met CEOs, billionaires, con men, and socialites. I've had knives pulled on me and phones thrown at me. It's been quite a ride.

But the time for looking back is over. I've had a proud, successful career, but I have no intention of resting on my laurels. My plan is to remain a working lawyer until I drop. My "sabbatical" was relaxing, but relaxing isn't really my kind of thing. I can't even imagine retiring. I'm back in business, there are clients waiting, and I have work to do.

— The End —

Photos

Sydney & Bertha, Noel Gage's parents

Leslie age 8 and Noel age 3

Noel 3-2-1942 in Newburgh NY

Camp Birchwood

Childhood Home

Young Noel - High School

Judge Hilda R. Gage

Chief Ed Ritenour

Leonard Lemberg

Head on a Platter Statue